SpringerBriefs in Computer Science

SpringerBriefs present concise summaries of cutting-edge research and practical applications across a wide spectrum of fields. Featuring compact volumes of 50 to 125 pages, the series covers a range of content from professional to academic.

Typical topics might include:

- A bridge between new research results, as published in journal articles, and a contextual literature review
- A snapshot of a hot or emerging topic
- An in-depth case study or clinical example
- A presentation of core concepts that students must understand in order to make independent contributions

Briefs allow authors to present their ideas and readers to absorb them with minimal time investment. Briefs will be published as part of Springer's eBook collection, with millions of users worldwide. In addition, Briefs will be available for individual print and electronic purchase. Briefs are characterized by fast, global electronic dissemination, standard publishing contracts, easy-to-use manuscript preparation and formatting guidelines, and expedited production schedules. We aim for publication 8–12 weeks after acceptance. Both solicited and unsolicited manuscripts are considered for publication in this series.

**Indexing: This series is indexed in Scopus and zbMATH **

More information about this series at http://www.springer.com/series/10028

Máté Horváth · Levente Buttyán

Cryptographic Obfuscation

A Survey

Máté Horváth
Department of Networked
Systems and Services
Budapest University of Technology
and Economics (BME-HIT)
Budapest, Hungary

Levente Buttyán
Department of Networked
Systems and Services
Budapest University of Technology
and Economics (BME-HIT)
Budapest, Hungary

ISSN 2191-5768   ISSN 2191-5776 (electronic)
SpringerBriefs in Computer Science
ISBN 978-3-319-98040-9   ISBN 978-3-319-98041-6 (eBook)
https://doi.org/10.1007/978-3-319-98041-6

This Springer imprint is published by the registered company Springer Nature Switzerland AG
The registered company address is: Gewerbestrasse 11, 6330 Cham, Switzerland

To our teachers

Preface

"The Lord searches every heart and understands every desire and every thought."

1 Chronicles 28:9, NIV

The ambitious goal of cryptographic obfuscation is to hide the operation of computer programs. Being an applied science, problems considered by cryptography are rarely investigated from a philosophical point of view but in the case of obfuscation, probably it worth spending some time considering the consequences of achieving this goal. The possibility of securely obfuscating arbitrary functions could radically change the relationship between humans and computer programs. Namely, it would imply losing our insight into the programs which we have had, at least in principle, since the writing of the first program code. While this change still seems to be futuristic, recent cryptographic advancements made it more probable than ever before.

In 2013 the breakthrough result of Garg, Gentry, Halevi, Raykova, Sahai and Waters (FOCS 2013) changed the previously pessimistic attitude towards general-purpose cryptographic obfuscation. Their finding was twofold. First, they managed to construct an obfuscator candidate that works for any function, which nonetheless was based on a rather idealistic assumption, and they showed a way to address the problem that had seemed impossible earlier. But what was probably even more important, they also demonstrated that their new tool is indeed useful and can help to solve other cryptographic problems as well. This latter observation was especially surprising as the security guarantee they achieved (called indistinguishability obfuscation) did not seem to have a practical relevance previously. An avalanche began and obfuscation became a central hub of cryptographic research. Cryptology ePrint Archive, the most active manuscript sharing forum of the community, counted over 190 related papers four years after the breakthrough, while before that fewer than 30 dealt with the topic. The potential realizability of such a powerful tool motivated a plethora of applications, including solutions for long-standing open problems, from almost all areas of cryptography. At the same time, intense development of candidate constructions started with the double goal of basing the security of obfuscation on solid foundations and turning its incredible overhead into tolerable.

While these goals were still not achieved when finalizing our manuscript, the "obfuscation-fever" has already led us much closer to the root of hardness behind encrypted computations. However, looking up and understanding the key thoughts from an already huge number of articles that themselves are looking for the right definitions, methods, and formulations can be really troublesome and time-consuming. This challenge, which we also had to face, motivated us to review the rapid development of candidate obfuscator constructions and organize the results of the first years since the breakthrough. As the field is still changing rapidly, our work is not intended to be a retrospection but rather a handrail for those who are fascinated by the incredible opportunities offered by obfuscation and would like to catch up with the latest results by understanding their background.

We hope that our survey can reflect the beauty of the field and the reader will find answers for many of his or her questions in it.

Budapest,   *Máté Horváth*
November 2018   *Levente Buttyán*

Acknowledgements

First of all, we would like to thank our families for their patience. In this regard, special thanks goes to Judit. We are grateful to Ágnes Kiss, Örs Rebák and members of the CrySyS Lab for their efforts to help us improve this work. We appreciate the valuable questions and remarks of Ryo Nishimaki, Ran Canetti, Zvika Brakerski and unknown reviewers that either highlighted flaws in earlier versions of our manuscript or helped us to better understand certain problems. Finally, we would also like to acknowledge the support of the National Research, Development and Innovation Office – NKFIH of Hungary under grant contract no. 116675 (K).

Contents

Glossary

annihilating polynomial   A polynomial ρ is called the annihilating polynomial of a matrix A if $\rho(A) = 0$.

black-box technique   When constructing (or separating, i.e. proving the impossibility of a reduction) one cryptographic primitive $\mathcal{P}$ from another one $\mathcal{Q}$, and we treat both $\mathcal{Q}$ and the adversary $\mathcal{A}$ as a black box (i.e. their code is not used), we say that the reduction from $\mathcal{P}$ to $\mathcal{Q}$ (or their separation) is black-box. Based on the extent of non-black-box techniques, several other notions of reducibility were defined by [RTV04] and refined by [BBF13].

branching program   A branching program (BP) (a.k.a. binary decision diagram) is a DAG consisting of inner nodes of fan-out 2 labelled by Boolean variables l_i, including the source node (fan-in 0) and sinks of fan-out 0, labelled 0 or 1. The computation starts at the source and, at each node l_i, one proceeds to the other edge with label 0 if the ith input bit $x_i = 0$ or to the other if $x_i = 1$. The BP computes f if, for an input x, it reaches a sink, labelled by $f(x)$. A BP is *layered* if the nodes are partitioned into layers where the source is in the first layer and the sinks are in the last, and edges go only between nodes in consecutive layers. A permutation BP is a layered BP where all the nodes of a layer observe the same variable and the edges between any pair of consecutive layers form a permutation of the vertices (for any setting of the variables). See [Mit15, §5.8.1] and [Weg00].

coAM The complexity class **coAM** is the complement of **AM**, which is the set of decision problems which are decidable in polynomial-time by a so-called Arthur–Merlin protocol (a specific interactive proof system) with two messages. See [AKG17].

CRS model In the common reference string (CRS) model, it is assumed that everyone has access to a public string that is drawn from a predetermined distribution during a set-up phase.

factoring The standard assumption of the hardness of factoring [Rab79] states that given $N = p_1 \cdots p_q$, where all p_i are random prime numbers of a given size, it is hard to find K such that $\gcd(K, N) \notin \{1, N\}$.

knowledge assumption "Knowledge or extractability assumptions capture our belief that certain computational tasks can be done efficiently only by going through certain specific intermediate stages and generating some specific kinds of intermediate values. /.../ Though these assumptions do not fall in the class of falsifiable assumptions [Nao03], these have been proven secure against generic algorithms, thus offering some evidence of validity." [GS14, §8 (full version)]

learning with errors The search/decisional learning with errors (LWE) assumption of [Reg05] states that it is hard to recover/distinguish a secret random vector $x \in \mathbb{Z}_p^n$ given noisy linear equations on it, i.e. given $y \in \mathbb{Z}_p^n$ and random $A \in \mathbb{Z}_p^{n \times m}$ such that $y = Ax + e \mod p$, where e is a random error vector of small magnitude. For its attractive features (e.g. suspected resistance to quantum attacks) and its connections to other assumptions, see [Pei16].

NC^0 The class functions (also called local functions) which are computable by constant-depth, bounded-fan-in circuits, meaning that each output bit can only depend on a constant number of input bits. See [AKG17].

NC^1 The class of polynomial-size circuits with logarithmic depth and bounded fan-in gates (more generally **NC^k** denotes the class of polynomial-size circuits of bounded fan-in having depth $O(\log^k n)$, where n is the input length). See [AKG17].

negligible function $\operatorname{neg}(n)$ is called negligible if it grows more slowly than any polynomial, i.e. $\forall c \in \mathbb{N}, \exists n_0 \in \mathbb{N}$ such that $\forall n \geq n_0$: $\operatorname{neg}(n) < n^{-c}$.

NP   "**NP** is the class of decision problems solvable by a
                           non-deterministic polynomial-time TM such that if the
                           answer is 'yes,' at least one computation path accepts,
                           but if the answer is 'no,' all computation paths reject"
                           [AKG17].

NTRU   This is a public-key cryptosystem proposed by [HPS98]
                           that is a possible alternative to factorization and discrete-
                           log-based encryption schemes because of its efficiency
                           and the fact that it is not known to be vulnerable to quan-
                           tum attacks. [SS11] made it provably secure, assuming
                           the hardness of worst-case problems over ideal lattices.
                           The abbreviation refers to an Nth-degree *tru*ncated poly-
                           nomial ring, the underlying algebraic structure on which
                           the cryptosystem is built.

one-way function   Informally speaking, a one-way function is a function
                           that is easy to evaluate but hard to invert (on average).
                           For further background, see [Gol06, §2].

one-way permutation   A one-way function that is a permutation (it is injective).

P   The class of decision problems solvable in polynomial-
                           time by a Turing machine. See [AKG17].

P/poly   The class of polynomial-size circuits with unbounded
                           depth (or, equivalently, polynomial-time TMs that take
                           advice of polynomial length). See [AKG17] and [Gol08,
                           §3.1].

proof system   A proof system consists of a *prover* and a *verifier*, where
                           the prover aims to convince the verifier of a true state-
                           ment. It is called "non-interactive" if the whole interac-
                           tion between the parties is one message from the prover
                           to the verifier. For details of the specific non-interactive
                           witness-indistinguishable proofs used in the bootstrap-
                           ping of obfuscation, see [FS90] and [GGH$^+$13b, §B.4];
                           for proof systems in general, see [Gol06, §4.10].

random oracle model   In this model, the cryptographic hash function is replaced
                           by its ideal functionality: a truly random function, called
                           a random oracle.

SAT   The Boolean satisfiability problem, which asks if there
                           exists an assignment of variables in a given Boolean for-
                           mula such that it evaluates to 1.

signature scheme   A signature scheme consists of three efficient algorithms:
                           KeyGen (which outputs a signing and a verification key,
                           sk and vk, respectively), Sign (which prepares a signature
                           s for a message m, using sk), and verification (which on
                           input (m, s) and vk outputs 1 if s is a valid signature of m
                           under sk, and rejects otherwise). For the definition of its
                           security, see the summary in [Gol06, §B.2].

SNARG

Succinct non-interactive arguments (SNARG) is a computationally sound (i.e. it is computationally infeasible to prove an assertion that is not true) proof system with short proofs for an NP-language. See [DSB17].

SNARK

Succinct non-interactive argument of knowledge (SNARK) is a SNARG system with the additional property that the correctness of a SNARK proof guarantees that the prover "knows" a witness to the statement with overwhelming probability. For details, see [BCC$^+$17, DSB17].

standard model

In the standard, or plain, model, we assume that the adversary is limited only by the available amount of time and computational power.

TC^0

TC^0 $\subseteq$ **NC^1** is the class of all Boolean circuits with constant depth and polynomial size, containing only unbounded-fan-in AND gates, OR gates, NOT gates, and threshold gates. See [AKG17].

trapdoor permutation

Intuitively, this is a one-way permutation with the extra property that, given some auxiliary information (the trapdoor), it is efficiently invertible. See [Gol06, §2.4.4].

Turing machine

The model of Turing machines captures all computational tasks that can be solved by classical computers. For details, see e.g. [Gol08, §1.2.3.2].

Acronyms

AS	Ananth–Sahai assumption
BGKPS	ideal graded encoding scheme (GES) model proposed by [BGK$^+$14] (see Table 2.4)
BP	branching program
BPO	best-possible obfuscation
BR	ideal GES model proposed by [BR13] (see Table 2.4)
BSH	bounded speedup hypothesis
BSH$'$	parametrized bounded speedup hypothesis
CCA	chosen ciphertext attack model
CDH	computational Diffie–Hellman problem
CLT13	candidate GES type based on [CLT13]
CPA	chosen plaintext attack model
CRS	common reference string (see Glossary)
CRT	Chinese remainder theorem
d-MBP	dual-input matrix branching program (MBP)
DAG	directed acyclic graph
DDH	decisional Diffie–Hellman problem
DES	data encryption standard
DiO	differing-input obfuscation
Dlog	discrete logarithm problem
dRE	decomposable randomized encoding
EPI	equivalent program indistinguishability
ETH	exponential time hypothesis
(P_1, P_2, P_3, P_4)-FE	functional encryption with the properties defined in §2.2.2
FE	functional encryption
FHE	fully homomorphic encryption
$\mathcal{F}_{\text{Lin}}$	function class defined by [Lin16] (see §4.4.1)
gcd	greatest common divisor
GCMM	generic coloured matrix model of [GGH$^+$13b]

GES	graded encoding scheme
GGH13	candidate GES type based on [GGH13a]
GGH15	candidate GES type based on [GGH15]
GGHZ	the assumption proposed by [GGHZ16]
GGM	generic group model
gMBP	generalized MBP of [BMSZ16]
GMM+	"weak" ideal GES model proposed by [GMM$^+$16] (see Table 2.4)
IBE	identity-based encryption
iO	indistinguishability obfuscation
IPFE	inner-product functional encryption
jSXDH	joint SXDH
LWE	learning with errors (see the Glossary)
MBP	matrix branching program
MIFE	multi-input functional encryption
ML	machine learning
MMap	multilinear map
MPC	secure multi-party computation
MSE	multilinear subgroup elimination assumption
MSW-1	"multiplication restricted" ideal GES model of [MSW15] (see Table 2.4)
MSW-2	"non-restricted" ideal GES model of [MSW15] (see Table 2.4)
MSZ	"weak" ideal GES model proposed by [MSZ16] (see Table 2.4)
NIWI	non-interactive witness-indistinguishable proofs
NMiO	neighbouring-matrix iO
OWF	one-way function (see the Glossary)
PAFE	projective arithmetic functional encryption
pdRE	program-decomposable randomized encoding
PiO	probabilistic indistinguishability obfuscation (iO)
pk-FE	public-key functional encryption
PKE	public-key encryption
PPRF	puncturable pseudo-random function
PPT	probabilistic polynomial time
PRF	pseudo-random function
PRG	pseudo-random generator
PRG$^{X=z}$	polynomial-stretch pseudo-random generator (PRG) with complexity z according to the complexity measure X (see §2.2.5)
RAM	random access machine
RE	randomized encoding
rMBP	relaxed MBP of [AGIS14]
ROM	random oracle model (see the Glossary)
SD	subgroup decision assumption

SE	slotted encoding
SHE	somewhat homomorphic encryption
SiO	strong iO
sk-FE	secret-key functional encryption
SNARG	succinct non-interactive argument (see the Glossary)
SNARK	succinct non-interactive argument of knowledge (see the Glossary)
SSGES	semantic security of GESs
SSGES'	sub-exponential semantic security of GESs
SXDH	symmetric external Diffie–Hellman assumption
SXiO	strong exponentially efficient iO (XiO)
SXiO'	strong XiO with compression factor only slightly smaller than 1
TM	Turing machine (Glossary)
UC	universal circuit
VBB	virtual black-box
VGB	virtual grey-box
WBC	white-box cryptography
XiO	exponentially efficient iO

Chapter 1
Introduction

1.1 Goals and Challenges

"Cryptography is about replacing trust with mathematics."[1] Cryptographic obfuscation – one of cryptography's aspiring branches, the subject of this study – focuses on the possibility of replacing *trust in software users* with mathematics. From another perspective, research on obfuscation seeks the answer to the question of whether all possible descriptions of a computer program are inherently understandable or there exist methods that enable programs to preserve their secrets.

Everyday experience might suggest a positive answer as anyone who has ever tried to understand an unfamiliar program code has discovered that finding out how a program works can be really difficult. Even famous results from the theory of computation seem to suggest that transparency is not the natural state of programs. For instance, the non-decidability of the halting problem [Tur36] indicates that, based on a description of an arbitrary program and an input to it, we cannot always determine whether or not it will ever terminate. Rice's theorem [Ric53] is even more suggestive. Intuitively, it says that there is no general method to check whether a program performs a specific (non-trivial) task. It is tempting to conclude that sufficiently complex programs are impossible to understand, and thus information can be hidden in them. Note, however, that these results are implied even by a single contrived example and do not say anything about other programs. In fact, the ambitious goal of general-purpose obfuscation is to argue that the inner workings of *all* interesting programs can be hidden from anyone with full access to the program.

But what makes a program interesting from the viewpoint of obfuscation? There are programs that we call "learnable" because, by executing them on sufficiently many inputs, the program can be efficiently reconstructed merely from the resulting input–output pairs. "Hello, world" is the simplest example, where any attempt to hide something related to the functionality is pointless, because by its nature, it reveals entirely how it works. But it is not only trivial programs of no utility that can be learnable. [TZJ+16], for instance, have shown that black-box access to confiden-

---

[1] According to the neat definition of Boaz Barak [Bar16b].

© The Author(s), under exclusive licence to Springer Nature Switzerland AG 2020
M. Horváth and L. Buttyán, *Cryptographic Obfuscation*, SpringerBriefs
in Computer Science, https://doi.org/10.1007/978-3-319-98041-6_1

tial machine learning (ML) models is sufficient for the duplication (in other words, stealing) of the model without prior knowledge of any parameters or the training data. Such attacks are called "model extraction", and are applicable to the real-life models that are deployed with publicly available query interfaces such as Amazon Machine Learning [Ama] or BigML [Big]. As the attack makes no use of the source code of the ML model, any countermeasures would try in vain to hide the details of the model, just as in the case of any other learnable programs. On the other hand, there are plenty of other programs which cannot be reverse-engineered in a black-box way (e.g. plaintext–ciphertext pairs of a symmetric-key encryption algorithm do not leak the key), and in the rest of this paper, we focus on these unlearnable programs.

In fact, the huge demand for preventing reverse-engineering and for intellectual property protection of software has made heuristic solutions prevalent in practice, as cryptography has not been able to offer viable methods for these problems up until now. In software engineering, the term "code obfuscation" refers to techniques that aim to make source code (or machine code) hard to understand both for humans and for automated tools. However, the success of this effort is rather doubtful, and depends largely on the state of the arms race between code obfuscator tools and code analysis techniques. The reason behind this is that all code obfuscation techniques rely on security via obscurity, contradicting the basic principles of cryptography, where it is always assumed that "the enemy knows the system being used" [Sha49], and precisely formulated security guarantees are expected to be fulfilled. One of the most urgent tasks of cryptography is to provide usable techniques that meet some rigorous definitions of obfuscation security in order to exceed the current vague methods, just like what has happened in the case of securing communications by means of real cryptographic algorithms in the 20th century. This survey is dedicated to the first steps in this process; for further details of the known techniques in daily use, we refer to the first taxonomy [CTL97] and recent surveys [SKK+16, XZKL17].

Before turning towards the cryptographic approach, we have to make it clear that programs are characterized by their functionality, i.e. their input–output behaviour, and their description, which varies with the chosen language and also with the programmer who prepared the program. Obfuscation is a program transformation (a compiler) denoted by $\mathcal{O}$, that preserves the functionality of the input program but alters its description such that the transformation does not affect the performance significantly (a moderate slowdown can be tolerated), and the resulting description is in some sense unintelligible. The goal of cryptography is to give a rigorous yet realizable definition for the latter elusive requirement. An intuitive but very strict formulation of unintelligibility is to expect that a program description reveals no more information about the program than does its functionality, which is public anyway. Practically, for this, the program needs to work as a virtual black box (hence the name virtual black-box (VBB) obfuscation [BGI+01]) that reveals the output for each queried input, but nothing more. A naive attempt to realize a VBB-secure obfuscator that comes to mind is to describe the program by its lookup table, which contains all possible input–output pairs but nothing more, thus satisfying the security requirement. Unfortunately, the storage requirement of this approach is exponentially large for most useful programs, hence making it completely impractical. It also violates the slowdown requirement of obfuscation, as returning an output on some input would require a lookup operation in that exponentially large storage. This relationship between (in)efficiency and (in)security illustrates the inevitable challenge that obfuscation has to face.[2] Namely, compression of a lookup table works by exploiting, and thus, revealing the structure of the function or program. From this perspective, the study of obfuscation asks whether it is possible to represent programs concisely without entirely revealing their structure to a computationally bounded adversary.

1.2 Related Concepts – A Brief Comparison

Table 1.1: Comparison with related concepts in cryptography that aim to secure computation without relying on trusted hardware.

	Obfus-cation	FHE	FE	MPC	RE or Garbling	GES
Input	Plaintext	Ciphertext	Ciphertext	Ciphertext	Ciphertext	Ciphertext
Output	Plaintext	Ciphertext	Plaintext	Plaintext	Plaintext	Ciphertext or 0
No. of possible evaluations	Any	Any	Any	1	1	Any
Is the function public?	No	Yes	Usually yes	Yes	No	Yes

Before going ahead, let us illustrate the challenges of obfuscation from yet another angle. If we relax the problem to hiding only a single value that is an integral part of the program (e.g. a key) instead of the entire inner structure, we still have to find a way to use this value in order to produce the output while maintaining its security throughout the whole computation. This scenario is reminiscent of securing computation on hidden data, for which several solutions have been proposed in the literature. In order to prevent misconceptions about the goal of general-purpose obfuscation, we will briefly compare it with related concepts, highlighting the similarities and the differences (see Table 1.1). As it will turn out later, understanding the similarities can get us closer to the realization of obfuscation, but computation on hidden data is not equivalent to program obfuscation.

White-box cryptography (WBC).   WBC is a strict attack model for cryptographic primitives, in which the endpoints of communication are not assumed to be trusted, contrary to traditional black-box models (e.g. CPA, CCA). In this model, the attacker can inspect and even modify the implemented code and also the execution environment of a primitive, for example a block cipher, with the embedded secret key. The theoretical foundations of WBC were investigated in

---

[2] This view of the problem was taken from the inspiring talk of Amit Sahai [Sah14].

[SWP09, Wys09, DLPR13], while the first white-box implementation (for fixed-key DES) was proposed by [CEJvO02] and was broken almost immediately [JBF02], just like other subsequent proposals (see [BHMT16, §2] and references therein). Clearly, any prospective "WBC compiler" that turns a primitive with black-box-model security into a white-box-secure one is essentially a special-purpose obfuscator for the given functionality, and thus the problem of constructing WBC-secure primitives can be regarded as a special case of general-purpose obfuscation. (Note, however, that WBC is an attack model in which secure solutions can also be built directly, without using a compiler.)

Secure multi-party computation (MPC).   MPC is aimed at enabling n parties to jointly compute an n-variate function f on their inputs (often through several rounds of *interaction*), without revealing their inputs to the other parties. Since the publication of the seminal work of Yao [Yao82], various aspects of this problem have been investigated, and several elegant solutions (both theoretical and practical) have been proposed [LP09b]. Compared with obfuscation, MPC can only guarantee the security of a jointly executed computation if at least one of the parties is honest, while obfuscation needs to achieve this in the presence of a single untrusted party. Nevertheless, MPC and obfuscation are closely related problems (see [CGP15, BGI+14a]), which is also reflected by the fact that the starting point of many candidate obfuscator schemes is Kilian's protocol for secure two-party computation [Kil88].

Garbled circuits and randomized encodings (REs).   The famous solution of Yao for secure two-party computation with his so-called "garbled circuits" [Yao86, LP09a] is puzzling from the perspective of obfuscation, because by using the garbling of a circuit C (representing some function) and an encoding of an input x, $C(x)$ can be computed, but nothing else, which also coincides with the functionality of RE (see §2.2.3). This is truly the goal of obfuscation as well, although garbling and RE are restricted to one-time use, meaning that new garblings are necessary for different inputs. As [GKP+13] pointed out, even reusable garbled circuits are not alone enough to achieve obfuscation. Regardless of the one-time use limitation, RE has a significant role in the realization of obfuscation, which we discuss in §4.

Fully homomorphic encryption (FHE).   The holy grail of cryptography, as FHE is often referred to [Wu15], enables one to compute arbitrary functions on hidden data. While when using traditional cryptosystems one has to sacrifice flexible handling of data in order to secure it, FHE allows one to execute *any* computation on encrypted data x, without decryption or even knowing the secret key. The output of such homomorphic evaluation of some function f results in a valid ciphertext that, when decrypted with the secret key, gives the correct result $f(x)$ of the computation. However, in our previous example of hiding only a single key in a program while keeping it functional, we needed exactly to compute some (public) function on the hidden key, but FHE cannot help us to do this, because either we would not be able to decrypt the resulting output in the absence of the secret key or if we had the key, the secret itself would become decryptable. Another issue is that obfuscation tries to hide the evaluated function, while FHE works with public functions. In spite of the differences, FHE is also an important tool of current obfuscation constructions, on which we elaborate further in §2.2.1 and §4.1.1–4.1.2.

Graded encoding schemes (GESs).   A GES [GGH13a], a generalization of a bilinear pairing, is closely related to somewhat homomorphic encryption (SHE) as – in contrast to FHE – both permit only a limited number of homomorphic operations on ciphertexts, with some additional constraints in the case of GESs. Importantly, while this limitation is part of the functionality in the first case, in the other case it is, rather, a functionality defect. Another key difference is that while SHE and FHE allow access to the result of the computation in an all-or-nothing manner (based on the possession of a decryption key), GESs are able to provide very restricted information about the result, namely whether it is zero or not. This little piece of information turns out to be crucial and makes this primitive extremely powerful. In §2.2.4, we elaborate more on this, and at this point highlight only that GESs are the main ingredient of all current obfuscation schemes, even if alone they can support only limited computations with partial information about the output.

Functional encryption (FE).   The concept of FE opens the door to authorizable computation on encrypted data with plaintext output. This is carried out by integrating the function into the secret key such that decryption with this "functional key" reveals no more information than the result of the computation of the function on the data behind the ciphertext. This functionality would coincide with that of an obfuscator if FE was a public-key scheme and the function could be hidden in the secret key. Note that the obfuscation of f could consist of the FE public key and a secret key for f, and the execution of this obfuscation would involve the encryption of the input with the public key and the decryption of the resulting ciphertext with the functional key. Unfortunately, FE with such ideal properties has not been realized yet; moreover, several impossibility results are known for powerful variants [AGVW13, GGG$^+$14]. Nevertheless, weaker forms of FE are also closely connected to obfuscation, and even if they do not imply it directly, they have a key role in several constructions which we discuss in §4 and §6 after introducing FE in more detail in §2.2.2.

1.3 The Cryptographic Approach

Having seen the challenges of realizing obfuscation and also plenty of examples of related concepts (either from cryptography or from software engineering), we would now like to give an intuition of the cryptographic approach to constructing obfuscators. For this, we use the analogy with data encryption, as obfuscation can be interpreted as the encryption of programs or functions (see Table 1.2 for a concise comparison). The first observation which is evident from this comparison is that we need to represent programs in a language that mathematics can handle (recall that we would like to substitute trust with mathematics). As programming languages are designed to be intuitive for humans, they are inappropriate for our purpose (just as human-readable data formats do not necessarily coincide with the format used during encryption). In the case of the encryption of programs, the plaintext space corresponds to a computational model (most often, the circuit model is used in this paper), in which we represent the program to be obfuscated. Unfortunately, in the case of complex programs, this language change seems to be troublesome today, or at least not as evident as representing data in a binary format for the purpose of encryption. Note, however, that before the age of computers, finding a good representation of data for encryption purposes was problematic too.

Regarding security, we have already mentioned the very strong and intuitive VBB paradigm. However, VBB was proven to be impossible to realize in general [BGI+01] (see §3.1.3). Current obfuscator candidates realize another security notion instead, called indistinguishability obfuscation (iO), that can be viewed as an analogue of semantic security [GM82]. The security requirement considers two different descriptions P_1 and P_2 (which have roughly the same size) of the same program, the iO obfuscations of which should be indistinguishable. Recall that semantic security considers two distinct messages (of the same size) and requires that their encryptions are indistinguishable. Noticeably, the two concepts have the same flavour; the difference lies in the nature of the objects to be hidden. In contrast to messages, program descriptions have an extra aspect, their functionality, that helps in distinction. Since obfuscation is not intended to hide the input–output behaviour, we are interested in distinguishability based solely on the description, so it is straightforward to investigate programs with the same functionality. We say that an obfuscator/encryption scheme is iO/semantically secure if the above requirements hold for all programs/messages (from a given program family/message space). Unfortunately, it is harder to see what kind of security (if any) is guaranteed by the iO notion. Indeed, the following transformation fulfils the iO security requirement, but may not help in hiding anything.

Example 1.1 ([BGI+01]). Let the iO obfuscation of a program P be the lexicographically first program description of size $|P|$ that computes the same function as P.

This clearly *inefficient* obfuscator can be seen as a "pseudo-canonicalizer" that possibly outputs a totally understandable description. However, it has been shown [GR07] that for *efficient* obfuscators, the iO notion indeed guarantees security, and, what is more, it achieves the maximum that we can hope for (see §3.2.2 for details). The crux is that the definition of iO is not explicit about the hidden information. One way of bridging this gap in the application of such obfuscators is via designing programs that inherently have multiple forms, differing in essence. The iO obfuscation of these implies that the essential difference becomes hidden in the obfuscated programs as we cannot tell them apart (we are going to see an example of this method in §4.1.2).

The last but at the same time the most important question is *how to realize an iO obfuscator?* The principle is again analogous to encryption, as in obfuscation we also utilize randomization. However, this randomization is much more involved owing to the constraint that the obfuscated program must remain functional for anyone, so the cancellation of random values cannot be tied to the knowledge of a secret key. Instead, the criterion for the elimination of randomness is that one can execute all legitimate steps of the program such that every honest evaluation leads to the correct output, but even the tiniest deviation from the predetermined steps results only in garbage.

Implementing this high-level idea for arbitrary programs is an open problem at the time of writing. Current obfuscator candidates are therefore designed in two separate steps. One of them is called bootstrapping that attempts to simplify the task by invoking related tools of cryptography. Currently, two main branches of bootstrapping techniques are known. One assumes the existence of a restricted obfuscator, called core-obfuscator and amplifies it, the other builds on a certain FE scheme for some limited class of functions in order to achieve general-purpose iO obfuscation. These techniques are summarized in §4 and in Fig. 4.1. The other step is to construct these primitives, which actually necessitates the use of GESs, a poorly understood object with known (and most probably with still not revealed) vulnerabilities, which threaten the security of today's obfuscators as well. We investigate the possible realizations of core-obfuscators and bootstrappable FE in §5–6 and summarize the different solutions in Tables 5.1 and 6.1 respectively. The uncertainty around the realizability of general-purpose iO motivated the study of obfuscator combiners, aiming to transform several obfuscators with uncertain security into a provably secure one. In §7, we close our survey with these results.

Table 1.2: A high-level comparison of the security of data encryption and obfuscation, which can be viewed as encryption of programs (or functions).

	Data encryption	Program obfuscation
Representation	Binary/group element/...	Circuit/TM/RAM/...
Security definition	Semantic security: given any M_0, M_1 ($|M_0| = |M_1|$) $\text{Enc}(M_0) \sim \text{Enc}(M_1)$	iO: given any $P_1 = P_2$ ($|P_1| = |P_2|$) $\mathcal{O}_{iO}[P_1] \sim \mathcal{O}_{iO}[P_2]$
Information is hidden via	Randomization	Randomization
Randomness is cancelled by	Using a secret key	Performing *all legitimate* steps of the program

1.4 Milestones in Cryptographic Obfuscation

For completeness, we will go through the most important milestones in the history of obfuscation from the beginning up to the time of writing. Like most cryptographic problems, obfuscation appeared first in the seminal work of Diffie and Hellman [DH76] from 1976. They devised the use of a so-called "one-way compiler" to convert private-key cryptosystems to public-key ones by obfuscating the encryption algorithm with a hard-coded secret key and using the resulting program as the public key. More than 20 years passed – during which the resulting public-key encryption (PKE) revolutionized cryptography – before Canetti showed how to obfuscate point functions (which output 0 on every input except one of them, for which they return 1), although in a different context under the name "oracle hashing" [Can97].

The formal study of the problem was initiated by Hada [Had00] and Barak et al. [BGI$^+$01]. The latter publication introduced both of the VBB and iO security notions mentioned above, immediately proving that VBB is too strong to be realizable for arbitrary programs. With an impossibility result and seemingly too weak notions as alternatives (see §3 for further attempts), the study of obfuscation turned towards directions that tried to evade the impossibility result but still stick to the intuitive VBB paradigm, namely dealing with specific functions (e.g. the point functions mentioned [LPS04, Wee05], vote mixing [AW07], re-encryption [HRSV11], and d-CNF formulas [BR14a]), and using trusted hardware in realizing obfuscation [BCG$^+$11, GIS$^+$10].

In 2013, the first candidate multilinear maps (a.k.a. GESs) of [GGH13a] broadened the toolbox of cryptography, paving the way for the breakthrough candidate iO obfuscator of Garg et al. [GGH$^+$13b]. The subsequent work of Sahai and Waters [SW14] gave rise to a plethora of applications of iO through their "punctured programming" technique, which highlighted the suggestion that with some extra effort in program design, there is huge potential in iO. A rapid and enthusiastic development of iO candidates followed (which we review in §5.1–5.2), the results of which became dubious as a result of the increasing number of attacks on the underlying GES (see Table 2.2 later). These so-called "zeroizing attacks" do not threaten obfuscation directly, but, as it turned out, they soon led to attacks on obfuscation as well (we discuss these and the proposed countermeasures in §5.3).

The subsequent milestone was the radically new bootstrapping approach of [AJ15, BV15], which built iO from FE and not from a limited obfuscator as in previous work, notably extending the list of primitives whose secure realizations imply iO (see Fig. 4.1 later). Making use of these new opportunities, Lin [Lin16] initiated the study of decreasing the role of GESs in obfuscation, which led to a second generation of obfuscator candidates. While each candidate from the first generation required polynomial multilinearity, a new line of research, which we introduce in §4.4 and §6, managed to reduce this to different constants. Our work focuses on the development of these two generations of obfuscator candidates, which led to the following statement [LT17]: general-purpose iO exists assuming,

- the learning with errors (LWE) assumption holds;
- there exist so-called 3-linear maps (a generalization of bilinear maps; see §2.2.4);
- there exists a 3-block-local pseudo-random generator (PRG) with superlinear stretch (see §2.2.5).

While (to date) the viability of the last two assumptions is an open question, this result is a huge leap from the assumptions of the first candidate [GGH$^+$13b]. Still, the uncertainties around these assumptions reflect the fact that cryptographic obfuscation is still in its infancy. Indeed, several iO-sceptics believe that such a powerful tool cannot exist. At the same time, as Canetti states, "the study of iO has brought with it a whole new toolbox of techniques that are intriguing in their own right, and teach us about the power and limitations of working with encrypted computations" [Can15].

For completeness, we note that after our work a third generation of iO candidates has appeared [Agr18, AJS18, LM18]. These results manage to entirely eliminate the need for the poorly understood multilinear maps, but still rely heavily on various pseudo-random objects, the existence of which needs to be verified by future work.

1.5 This Survey and Related Literature

1.5.1 Organization.

Our paper is structured in the following way. §2 provides a brief introduction to the computational and security models, cryptographic primitives, and assumptions that are going to appear later on. §3 is dedicated to the different definitional approaches to obfuscation and to their relations and limitations. §4–6 deal with the realization of these definitions, especially iO. We introduce the current bootstrapping methods in §4, identifying so-called bootstrappable primitives, and in §5–6 we turn our attention towards the realizations of these. We close our survey by reviewing techniques that are aimed at improving the security of obfuscation by combining the various iO constructions introduced here.

1.5.2 Related Work.

Here we also recommend to the reader some related publications with a slightly different flavour and scope. In their review articles, Barak [Bar16a] and Garg et al. [GGH+16] gave a high-level introduction to the topic. Gentry [Gen14] investigated the nature of encrypted computation, focusing on homomorphic encryption. In his thesis, Mittelbach [Mit15, §5] gave a broad introduction to obfuscation, including also the details of several results used, and [Mit15, §6] surveyed results on point-function obfuscation.

1.5.3 On the Used Notation.

We denote an obfuscator, the central object in this work, by $\mathcal{O}$, in contrast to the big O notation for which we use $O(\cdot)$. If an obfuscator needs to be specified more precisely, the security achieved is indicated in a lower index, while the class of functions supported is specified in an upper index (e.g. $\mathcal{O}_{iO}^{NC^1}$ corresponds to an iO obfuscator for circuits in $\mathbf{NC^1}$). An obfuscated program is denoted by $\mathcal{O}[P]$ and can be executed on an input x, which is written as $\mathcal{O}[P](x)$. This highlights the meaning of the bracket type: an input in square brackets is always a program, and parentheses refer to some data input. As data inputs are usually meant to be binary sequences, the ith input bit position of x is denoted by x_i. Hard-coded, fixed parameters of a function, program, or algorithm are indicated by a lower index (e.g. $f_x(\cdot)$). We use $|C|$ to indicate the size of C and $|$ to denote concatenation. $\langle a,b \rangle$ refers to the inner product of a and b, while $\otimes$ indicates the tensor product. Indistinguishability is denoted by $\sim$, or by $\overset{c}{\sim}$ when computational indistinguishability is emphasized.

Chapter 2
Background

Before coming to the point, we first have to introduce the necessary background for our study. We start with the discussion of the first question that may possibly arise when dealing with programs, namely, *which representation of a computer program best serves our purposes?* We are going to use two models of computation, which are introduced in §2.1. In §2.2 we provide a brief introduction to the most important of the cryptographic primitives that we are going to use in subsequent sections. We close the section (§2.3) with a short discussion of the actual and desired assumptions behind obfuscation and the security models in which proofs are provided. For any other notion, concept, or primitive that appears in this paper but is not included in this section (because either it is regarded as standard in cryptography or is less important), we refer to the Glossary.

2.1 Representation of Programs

2.1.1 The Circuit Model of Computation

On the Choice of Program Representation.   Before turning our attention to the study of program obfuscation, we need to briefly elaborate on the choice of the computational model in which we are going to imagine programs. It turns out when considering functions which take programs as their input that it matters whether this input is represented in a uniform (e.g. a Turing machine (TM)) or in a non-uniform (e.g. circuits) model. Informally, in the former case the program is represented by a fixed set of instructions for all allowed inputs regardless of the input size, whereas, in a non-uniform model, the set of instructions can depend on the input size. From another perspective, the relationship between the two models may be more comprehensible: non-uniform computation can be captured either by circuits or, equivalently, by TMs that take "advice", meaning that, for each input length, the TM has access to a string that helps to solve the task. Specifically, the class **P/poly** includes all polynomial-time algorithms with input length n that have access to an advice string of length polynomial in n. Evidently, this shows that any uniform algorithm is also non-uniform with an empty advice string. Consequently, it might be possible that some forms of obfuscation are achievable for circuits but infeasible for TMs (indeed, this seems to be the case, as we will see in §3.1.4), whereas, if a TM obfuscator exists, then a circuit obfuscator also exists [BGI⁺01, Proposition 2.3]. Keeping these considerations in mind, from now on we are going to use circuits as the model of computation unless stated otherwise, because currently TM and random access machine (RAM) obfuscators[1] (which are outside of the scope of this paper) are also built from circuit obfuscators [BGL⁺15, CHJV14, KLW15, AJS17b].

About Circuits.   A circuit can be described by a directed acyclic graph (DAG) in which the vertices are of three types: sources (with in-degree zero), sinks (with out-degree zero), and internal vertices, called *gates*, which are associated with program steps; the edges between them identify their dependencies. The *fan-in/fan-out* of the circuit is the maximum in/out-degree of any vertex. The *depth* is defined as the longest directed path from any source to any sink. A circuit is called Boolean if its gates represent Boolean operations, while arithmetic circuits compute arithmetic functions. In this paper, we consider both types, but do not specify them when it is irrelevant or clear from the context. For the complexity classes considered, we refer to the Glossary. Further details of the circuit model can be found in [Gol08, §1.2.4.1].

Universal Circuits.   We briefly introduce universal circuits (UCs), which are "programmable" circuits in the sense that they receive the program description as an input. This means that the two inputs of a UC are the description[2] C' of a circuit C and the input x of C. Note that both C' and x denote ordinary bit strings. In this way, a Universal Circuit U_λ can be programmed to execute any circuit of a given size λ, such that $U_\lambda(C', x) = C(x)$, where $|C'| = \lambda$. We will use this concept several times, because it allows us to handle programs as data while preserving the opportunity to evaluate them on certain inputs. While this informal definition will suffice for our purposes, we refer to [Weg87, §4.8] and [KS16] for further details.

2.1.2 Matrix Branching Programs

The drawback of the circuit model of computation is that it seems very challenging to reason that something is indeed "hidden" in a circuit. The simplest way to avoid these difficulties is to change to a more structured model, such as that of branching

---

[1] We note that the definitions of TM obfuscation are almost identical to those which we present in §3, but, besides its size, the running time of a TM also has to be considered in the slowdown requirement.

[2] For simplicity, later on we will use the same notation for both a circuit and its description.

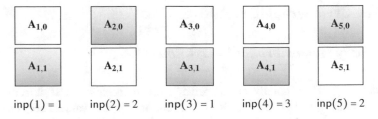

inp(1) = 1   inp(2) = 2   inp(3) = 1   inp(4) = 3   inp(5) = 2

Fig. 2.1: The computation of an MBP for input $x = (1,0,1)$ is $A_{1,1} \cdot A_{2,0} \cdot A_{3,1} \cdot A_{4,1} \cdot A_{5,0}$.

programs. Many current obfuscator candidates work for programs that are represented as matrix branching programs (MBPs). This is enabled by the well-known theorem of Barrington [Bar86], which provides a transformation of any depth-d fan-in-2 Boolean circuit C into an MBP of 5×5 matrices and of length at most 4^d, which computes the same function as the circuit C (note that for an $\mathbf{NC^1}$ circuit, the length remains polynomial in the depth d).

An MBP consists of a sequence of steps, represented by pairs of permutation matrices. In each step i, one input bit is examined and, depending on its value, one of a pair of matrices $(A_{i,0}, A_{i,1})$ is chosen. Finally, all these chosen matrices are multiplied, and the output of the MBP is said to be 1 if the resulting permutation is the identity and 0 otherwise.[3] The mapping between the n steps $(\{A_{i,0}, A_{i,1}\}_{i \in [n]})$ and ℓ input bits is described by the evaluation function $\mathsf{inp}(i) : [n] \to [\ell]$, which is also part of the MBP besides the matrices. For an intuitive example of the evaluation of an MBP, see Fig. 2.1.

Following [BGK+14], we use the name dual-input MBP (d-MBP) for MBPs in which the matrix choices of the steps depend on two input bits instead of a single bit. Accordingly, d-MBPs require two evaluation functions. Analogously to the single-input case, a d-MBP is computed by $\prod_{i=1}^{n} A_{i, x_{\mathsf{inp}_1(i)}, x_{\mathsf{inp}_2(i)}}$ on input x.

We remark that obfuscation transforms the matrices of an MBP but not its evaluation function, which may still contain some information about the program itself. This is not a problem in the case of *input-oblivious* MBPs, the evaluation function of which depends only on the input length of the circuit and not on the input values. Any MBP can be made input-oblivious (with an increase in length) by compressing all information about the program into the matrices; however, when only certain parts of a program (e.g. a key[4]) need to be hidden, we do not need this property.

---

[3] In general, any pair of permutation matrices A_1, A_2 can be specified to represent the outputs 0 and 1.

[4] A little more precisely, suppose that we have a publicly known circuit $C(.,.)$ with two inputs: a key K and another input. We obfuscate C somehow and fix the matrices that correspond to the bits of the key, and give out the obfuscation in this form (i.e. $\mathcal{O}[C_K](.)$ is published). Although the resulting obfuscated MBP is not input-oblivious, it hides the key that we want to keep secret.

2.2 The Cryptographic Primitives Used

2.2.1 Fully Homomorphic Encryption

The idea of FHE, originally called privacy homomorphism, was introduced by Rivest, Adleman, and Dertouzos [RAD78], and it aims to evaluate arbitrary functions on ciphertexts. More precisely, imagine a public-key encryption scheme with an additional algorithm for function evaluation, $\text{FHE.Eval}(C, \text{PK}, \text{CT}_x^{\text{PK}})$, which receives as input a circuit C, a public key PK, and a ciphertext, prepared using PK (i.e. $\text{FHE.Enc}(\text{PK}, x) = \text{CT}_x^{\text{PK}}$). The output of this algorithm is a new ciphertext, CT_y^{PK}. Moreover, it corresponds exactly to an encryption of the value $C(x) = y$ (i.e. $\text{FHE.Dec}(\text{SK}, \text{CT}_y^{\text{PK}}) = C(x) = y$), enabling computation on encrypted data. At this point, recall again the basic difference between FHE and obfuscation (Table 1.1): while obfuscation is aimed at hiding computation itself, working with ordinary inputs and outputs, FHE realizes computation on hidden data, resulting in a hidden output, meaning that it is not the function f that is concealed, but its effect on the concrete input.

The problem of building FHE was open for 30 years, until Gentry [Gen09] proposed the first solution, which was followed by rapid development leading to realizations under the LWE assumption. The main building block of FHE schemes is a so-called somewhat homomorphic encryption (SHE) scheme that is limited to executing a predetermined number of multiplications besides arbitrary additions. This functionality defect (compared with FHE) can actually be turned into a feature as we are going to see in §2.2.4.

Besides its extreme usefulness, for example in outsourced computation, FHE became a key ingredient of bootstrapping obfuscation (see §4.1), although its efficiency is still an issue in practice. For more elaborate studies of FHE, we refer to the surveys [Gen14, ABC+15].

2.2.2 Functional Encryption

[BSW11, O'N10] initiated the study of generalized encryption schemes, called FE, that support the use of restricted secret keys that allow the key holder only to learn specific functions of the encrypted data, and nothing more. FE integrates function evaluation into the decryption algorithm, enabling computation on hidden data. In contrast to FHE, this computation is allowed only to authorized users (who own the "functional secret key"), and its output is a plaintext. Both secret- and public-key variants are meaningful with the following syntax:

- $\text{FE.Setup}(1^\lambda)$ generates the master secret key MSK (and public key PK) based on the security parameter λ.

- FE.KeyGen(MSK, f) computes the functional secret key FSK_f, which can be used for decryption.
- FE.Enc(MSK, x) = CT_x encrypts some data x using MSK (or PK).
- FE.Dec($\mathsf{FSK}_f, \mathsf{CT}_x$) = $f(x)$ "decrypts" the ciphertext CT_x (in fact, it evaluates f on value x underlying CT_x).

Several flavours of secret- and public-key FE schemes have been investigated in the past, with various flavours of security, and varying efficiency, supporting different functions and even different numbers of possible functional key queries. Security can be defined both via indistinguishability and via simulation-based guarantees; however, for the latter, several impossibility results are known [BSW11, AGVW13], and in the rest of the paper, unless stated otherwise, we will always mean the former when referring to FE. Most often, we will consider FE schemes for general functions of some given complexity except for a specific functionality, namely the computation of inner products. In inner-product functional encryption (IPFE)[5] [ABCP15], ciphertexts and secret keys are associated with vectors, and decryption yields their inner product. Hiding the function (the vector) in the key is meaningful and also useful only in the secret-key setting, which was considered by [BJK15, DDM16, LV16a]. A common limitation of all current IPFE schemes is that the final result of the computation can only be obtained if it is contained in a polynomial-size range (e.g. in the case of Boolean outputs). This issue motivated the notion of projective arithmetic functional encryption (PAFE) [AS17], in which only partial decryption of ciphertexts is possible (explicitly) and an additional "recover" algorithm can restore linear functions of partially decrypted values.

Because of the diversity of FE schemes, we will use the parametrized notation (P_1, P_2, P_3, P_4)-FE to refer to different types of FE, for clarity. The meaning of the parameters is the following:

- $P_1 \in \{pk, sk, sk^*\}$ denotes whether the scheme is a public- or secret-key one and, in the latter case, whether the scheme is "puncturable" (sk^*), meaning roughly that a "punctured encryption key" can be prepared and that ciphertexts computed using this key and the ordinary key are indistinguishable even in the presence of both keys (for details see [BV15, §5.2] and [KNT18a, §5]).
- $P_2 \in \{1, c, m\}$ denotes the maximum number of supported functional secret-key queries (1 denotes a single-key scheme, c corresponds to a constant number of keys, and m refers to a "collusion-resistant" scheme that supports a polynomial number of keys in the security parameter).
- $P_3 \in \{1, c, m\}$ specifies the number of inputs to the function f (where 1 refers to a single input, c to some constant, and m to an arbitrary number). In the case of more than one input, the scheme is often referred to as multi-input functional encryption (MIFE).
- $P_4 \in \{NC, CS, WC, C, L\}$ refers to the efficiency of the encryption algorithm. NC means non-compact (there is no bound on the encryption time T_{Enc}); C

---

[5] Not to be confused with inner product predicate encryption [KSW13], where the goal of computing an inner product during decryption is not to obtain its result, but to determine whether the given key can decrypt a specific message or not.

means compact,[6] meaning that T_{Enc} is independent of the function size ($T_{\text{Enc}} <$ poly(n,λ) for input size n); in the case of a collusion-resistant scheme, CS refers to "collusion-succinctness" ($T_{\text{Enc}} <$ poly$(n,\lambda,|f|) \cdot m^{\gamma}$, where m is the maximum number of issuable functional keys and $\gamma < 1$); WC means weakly compact[7] ($T_{\text{Enc}} <$ poly$(n,\lambda) \cdot |f|^{1-\varepsilon}$ for some constant $\varepsilon < 1$) and L refers to linear efficiency ($T_{\text{Enc}} < n \cdot$ poly(λ) for input size n). When not stated otherwise, the ciphertext size has the same bound as the encryption time.

In §1.2, we have already hinted at the close connection of FE and obfuscation, on which we elaborate in §4.3–4.4.

2.2.3 Randomized Encodings

A demand for secure delegation of complex computations often emerges in cryptography. A typical scenario is when a computationally weak party wishes to "encode" a function f together with an input x to form a randomized $(\widehat{f,x})$ that can be securely forwarded for evaluation to an untrusted party with the necessary resources. Natural expectations are that the encoding procedure must be simpler – in some sense – than the computation that the weak party wants to execute, and that $f(x)$ must be computable from $(\widehat{f,x})$ but should not leak more information about f and x than $f(x)$ does. The concept of RE, introduced by [IK00], captures exactly this scenario. An RE scheme comprises two probabilistic polynomial time (PPT) algorithms:

- RE.Enc(C,x,r) generates the randomized encoding $(\widehat{C,x})$ of a circuit C on input x using some randomness r;
- RE.Eval$((\widehat{C,x}))$ is an evaluation function that allows the computation of $C(x)$ from the encoding $(\widehat{C,x})$.

The correctness and security requirements of the scheme say that a sample from the distribution $(\widehat{C,x})$ (induced by the random choice of r) must be decodable to $C(x)$ and an efficient simulator must be able to simulate the distribution $(\widehat{C,x})$ given merely $C(x)$.

To make this concept non-trivial and interesting, we also have to require that the complexity of RE.Enc is strictly smaller than the complexity of C. This feature of RE is used in a broad range of applications (including bootstrapping obfuscation; see §4.2) to reduce the complexity of different tasks (see also [App14b]). In the realization of RE, it is sufficient to use fairly standard techniques. Using Yao's garbled circuits [Yao86, LP09a] and a PRG in $\mathbf{NC^0}$, [AIK06] showed a realization of RE against computationally bounded adversaries for any polynomial-time computable function (any $C \in \mathbf{P/poly}$), where the encoding algorithm can be implemented by a constant-depth circuit. Another nice property of such garbling-based RE schemes is that the RE.Enc algorithm can be decomposed into polynomially many (in the

---

[6] Succinctness often refers to the same property in several articles.

[7] This is also called sub-linear compactness/succinctness.

size of the input circuit) components with constant size, meaning that each of them can be generated in time independent of the complexity of C. Practically, these components in Yao's garbled circuits are garbled gates. REs with this property are also called program-decomposable randomized encodings (pdREs) ([AJS15, §3.2], [LV16b, §2.4.1]). Note that the name decomposable randomized encoding (dRE) refers to a different property, namely that the encodings of C and x can be prepared independently, together constituting $\overline{(C,x)}$.

For a more elaborate discussion of randomized encodings, we refer to [App17].

2.2.4 Multilinear Maps and Graded Encodings

Hidden Computation with a Minimal Hint about the Result.   Assuming the hardness of the discrete logarithm problem (Dlog) enables restricted computation on hidden data. Knowing merely the encodings $g^{x_i} := [x_i]$ of $x_i \in \mathbb{Z}_p$ for some i (in some group G of prime order p with generator g), it is possible to compute linear functions of the plaintexts x_i in an *encrypted form*. For instance, one can determine $[\sum_i a_i \cdot x_i]$ for coefficients a_i of one's choice simply by computing $\prod_i [x_i]^{a_i}$. According to Dlog, it is hard to recover the result of the computation, although it is easy to decide whether it is zero ($[0] = g^0 = 1$) or whether it is equal to a certain value ($[x_i]/[x_j] = 1 \Leftrightarrow x_i - x_j = 0$). On the other hand, according to the computational Diffie–Hellman problem (CDH) it is not possible to compute quadratic functions such as $[x_i x_j]$ efficiently given only $[x_i]$ and $[x_j]$. Moreover, the decisional Diffie–Hellman problem (DDH) also states that even the recognition of the result of quadratic functions is hard, i.e. a claimed result $[x_i x_j]$ is hard to differentiate from the encoding of a random value $[r]$. These are widely used cryptographic assumptions; we mention only the simplest application, the two-party key exchange protocol of Diffie and Hellman.

Extension of the Computable Functions with Multilinear Maps (MMaps).   Intuitively, weakening the above strict constraint on the computable functions on hidden data can lead to the solution of more and more complex cryptographic tasks. Indeed, [Jou00] showed how to do a three-party key exchange (still in one round) using so-called bilinear maps. Denoting by $[x_i]_k = g_k^{x_i}$ the encoding of x_i in group G_k with generator g_k, such a mapping (also called a pairing) $e : G_1 \times G_2 \to G_3$ is linear in both of its variables, i.e. $e([x_i]_1, [x_j]_2) = [x_i x_j]_3$. Clearly, pairings allow the computation of quadratics on ciphertexts, but not cubics or higher-order functions. Note also that zero-testing of the result (in G_3) is still possible. This slightly increased freedom led to a vast number of applications in cryptography (see the survey of [Jou02]) and made Boneh and Silverberg [BS03] wonder about the far-reaching consequences of further generalization of bilinear maps. They proposed the notion of κ-MMaps $e : G_1 \times \cdots \times G_k \to G_{k+1}$, which would allow the computation of degree$-\kappa$ polynomials on encodings (possibly represented in identical or in

Table 2.1: Tag types and the compatibility constraints on them.

Tag type	Tag	Zero-test is allowed	Addition		Multiplication	
			IFF inputs	Output tag	IFF inputs	Output tag
Levels	$k,l \in \{1,2,\ldots,\kappa\}$	κ	$k = l$	l	$k \neq l \wedge (k+l) \leq \kappa$	$k+l$
Sets[a]	$S_k, S_l \subset \{1,2,\ldots,\kappa\}$	$\{1,2,\ldots,\kappa\}$	$S_k = S_l$	S_l	$S_k \cap S_l$	$S_k \cup S_l$
DAG[b]	Edges: $e_{i \rightarrow j}$	Any edges	Identical edges	As input	Consecutive edges: $e_{i \rightarrow j}, e_{j \rightarrow k}$	Edge $e_{i \rightarrow k}$

different groups, referred to as the symmetric or the asymmetric [Rot13] setting, respectively), but nothing more except testing the result for zero. To represent the usefulness of such maps, they showed how to realize key exchange between $(\kappa + 1)$ parties in one round. Unfortunately, they also managed to show that MMaps cannot be realized with the same techniques as pairings. The problem of constructing the imagined ideal (sometimes also called "clean" or "algebraic") MMaps is still open, even for $\kappa = 3$.

GESs: An Alternative to MMaps.   A possible circumvention of these difficulties became possible with the observation of [GGH13a] about the similarities of SHE and MMaps, which we have already described in the Introduction. The idea of those authors was to substitute the group elements $g_k^{x_i}$ from G_k that served as encodings of some value x_i with the corresponding ciphertexts of an SHE scheme (constructed from NTRU) in which a plaintext can be encrypted in different "levels". In their approach, $[x_i]_k$ is the level-k encryption of x_i using SHE, which leads to two important deviations from the MMaps of [BS03, Rot13]. First, the operations are not executed in one shot, but one by one under some restrictions (see Table 2.1). Second, the resulting ciphertexts contain some random "noise", ensuring the semantic security of SHE. As a result, encrypting the same value two times at the same level would result in different ciphertexts, thwarting the possibility of zero-testing. To handle this, [GGH13a] constructed a "handicapped" secret key (called zero-testing parameter) that does not allow the decryption of arbitrary ciphertext, but only encryptions of zero at a certain level. These authors called their "approximate" (or "noisy") MMap candidate graded encoding scheme and showed some evidence that generalizations of the DDH and CDH assumptions seem to hold for their GES construction (while other assumptions do not necessarily hold). GESs with these properties turned out to be extremely useful, for example enable n-party key exchange in one round [GGH13a] and many other applications including general-purpose indistinguishability obfuscation as was shown later by [GGH+13b].

[CLT13] proposed a second GES candidate based on FHE over the integers [vDGHV10, CCK+13], and [GGH15] used the FHE scheme of [GSW13] to build a GES.

At the time of writing, the above-mentioned candidates are the main GES types, but several variants of them have been proposed with various functionality and dif-

---

[a] This setting is often called "asymmetric" in contrast to the "symmetric" level tags.

[b] In this case, the edge tags and the constraints on them can be generalized for paths.

ferent intuitions about security (see Table 2.2), but without precise proofs of security (based on any standard assumptions), showing that our understanding of this primitive is still very limited.

For the purposes of this survey, it suffices to understand the functionality of GESs, which we present using the unified syntax proposed by Halevi.[8] A GES has three main parts (possibly realized by more algorithms in the various schemes):

Key generation. This takes as input a security parameter and the specification of the functionality, which is a description of so-called *tags* that will be associated with encrypted values. These are abstractions of the groups in which encodings are represented in the case of an ideal MMap (e.g. in the previous example, the tags were levels). The description includes the tag type, constraints on what operations are permitted on encodings with specific tags, and what will be the tag of the operation's output (see Table 2.1). The outputs of this phase are the public and secret parameters, and the latter also includes the plaintext space.

Encoding. This takes the secret parameter, an element of the plaintext space, and a tag, and returns an encoding of that element relative to the tag.

Operations. These are addition, multiplication, and zero-testing.[9]. The first two operate on two encodings with compatible tags and output an encoding of the sum or the product with the output tag. Zero-testing operates on one encoding with an allowed tag and returns a bit indicating whether the encoded value is zero.

We note that current GES constructions are subject to several attacks (see Table 2.2), but most of these affect only the public-key setting, where encodings (particularly of zero) can be prepared by the attacker. While this setting is typically needed for multi-party key exchange, for obfuscation we do not need public-key encoding and these attacks do not threaten obfuscation directly (see §5.3 for details). What is more, [PS15, AFH$^+$16, AFH$^+$15] showed that approximate MMaps can be constructed based on iO as well, meaning that we could use a vulnerable GES to construct iO that implies a GES which is not known to be insecure. This absurd situation reveals the serious holes in our current understanding of GESs (and iO), showing that there is still a huge amount of work left on this pillar of obfuscation.

On Composite-Order GESs. We note that [GLW14, Appendix B] showed that the candidate of [CLT13] is capable of implementation of approximate MMaps *over composite-order groups* that allow more powerful applications than prime-order ones. We elaborate on the source of this extra power briefly. Let $N = p_1 \cdot p_2 \cdots p_k$, where the elements of the product are distinct (co)primes. According to the Chinese remainder theorem (CRT), a plaintext value $x \in \mathbb{Z}_N$ implicitly determines $(x_1, \ldots, x_k) \in \mathbb{Z}_{p_1} \times \cdots \times \mathbb{Z}_{p_k}$ (where $x \equiv x_i \mod p_i$ for each $i \in \{1, \ldots, k\}$), and the encoding $[x]$ can also be viewed as $[x_1, \ldots, x_k]$ on which the operations act componentwise. This property allows information storage in all components while *en-*

---

[8] This viewpoint was sketched in an invited talk at CRYPTO 2015 and can be found in [Hal15].

[9] Sometimes there is an "extraction" operation as well for the same tags as for zero-testing but this returns a bit string.

Table 2.2: Summary of variants of and attacks on GESs. For a regularly maintained list of attacks against GESs, see [AD].

GES type	GGH13	CLT13	GGH15
Original candidate	[GGH13a]	[CLT13]	[GGH15]
Based on	Ideal lattices	CRT	Standard lattices
Suitable tag types	Levels/sets	Levels/sets	DAG
Variants	[LSS14, ACLL15, Hal15, GGHZ16, DGG+16, DPM17]	[BWZ14, GLW14, GGHZ16, CLT15]	[Hal15, Che16]
Attacks	[GGH13a, CGH+15, BGH+15, HJ16, ABD16, CJL16, CLLT16]	[LS14, CHL+15, CGH+15, CFL+16]	[GGH15, CLLT16]

forcing the performance of the same operations on each of them simultaneously. Furthermore, in the absence of the factorization of N, an adversary cannot easily eliminate one component of an encoded value without the elimination of all of them. An abstraction of these properties is called slotted encoding (SE), which [AS17] has shown to be realizable using *prime-order* MMaps (by extending the idea of dual vector spaces [OT08, BJK15]) when the required multilinearity κ is limited to being a constant.

2.2.5 Simple and Efficient Pseudo-Random Generators

A deterministic algorithm that expands the length of a random value such that the result is indistinguishable from uniformly random is called a PRG. This primitive plays a crucial role in several cryptographic tasks, including building iO obfuscators among others, so we summarize the relevant aspects of this field here. Informally, we are interested in functions $G: \{0,1\}^n \to \{0,1\}^{\ell(n)}$ that are pseudo-random, expanding, and simple. They are *pseudo-random* in the sense that $G(U_n) \stackrel{c}{\sim} U_{\ell(n)}$, where U_i denotes the uniform distribution of i bits. *Expanding* generally means $\ell(n) > n$, but our expectation is stronger, namely that G should stretch its input polynomially, i.e. $\ell(n) = n^{1+\alpha}$ for some constant $\alpha > 0$. *Simplicity* can be measured, for instance, by the so-called "locality" of the PRG, which is the maximum number of input bits that affect a single output bit of the PRG. If G can be computed by an $\mathbf{NC^0}$ circuit, it is also called "local", referring to the fact that its locality is constant. We mention two other complexity measures, block locality and degree, for PRGs. The notion of *block locality* was coined by [LT17] as a generalization of locality. These authors say that a PRG is (L, w)-blockwise local if its input can be divided into w-bit blocks and each output bit depends on at most L such blocks. Equivalently, $G: \mathbb{Z}_q^n \to \{0,1\}^{\ell(n)}$ holds, where $q = 2^w$. When the output bits are expressed as polynomials in the input bits (over the rationals), we call the maximum degree of these the ($\mathbb{Q}$-)*degree* of the PRG. Note that locality upper-bounds the $\mathbb{Q}$-degree.

In fact, fulfilling the above-listed requirements of pseudo-randomness with polynomial stretch and low locality is an important open problem, the solution of which would have a significant impact on obfuscation as well. The remarkable work of Applebaum et al. [AIK06] shows how to transform any PRG computable in $\mathbf{NC^1}$ to one in $\mathbf{NC^0}$ (with locality 4), providing local PRGs under practically all standard cryptographic assumptions. However, this transformation cannot achieve better than sub-linear stretch, irrespective of the stretch of the original PRG. On the negative side, [MST06] proved the impossibility of a polynomial-stretch PRG with locality less than 5.

The current candidates for polynomial-stretch PRGs with constant (blockwise) locality or $\mathbb{Q}$-degree are all rooted in the conjectured one-way function (OWF) of [Gol00], which is, however, not based on any standard assumptions. These "Goldreich-like" PRGs have the following structure. Let $P : \mathbb{Z}_q^k \to \{0,1\}$ be a predicate and H a bipartite graph with vertex sets named "input" and "output", with n and $\ell(n)$ vertices, respectively, where each node of the "output" set has k neighbours from the "input" set. The ith output bit of the PRG (mapping $\mathbb{Z}_q^k$ to $\{0,1\}^{\ell(n)}$) is determined by the predicate P, evaluated on the input bits that correspond to the neighbours of vertex i.

[OW14] showed some evidence for the security of a 5-local, Goldreich-like PRG with polynomial stretch, and [LV17] showed a candidate PRG with $\mathbb{Q}$-degree 4 and proved that 3 is a lower bound. Most recently, [BBKK17] pointed out that the stretch of any $(2,w)$-blockwise local PRG cannot go beyond $m = 2^w n$, and thus cannot be polynomial. For a more elaborate summary of local PRGs, we refer to [App16].

We are going to use the notation $\mathrm{PRG}^{X=z}$ to refer explicitly to a polynomial-stretch PRG with complexity z according to the complexity measure $X \in \{L, B, D\}$, where L denotes the locality, B is the block-locality, and D is the degree.

2.2.6 Puncturable Pseudo-Random Functions

One of the key ingredients of obfuscation (particularly iO [SW14]) applications is the simplest form of constrained pseudo-random functions (PRFs) [BW13, KPTZ13, BGI14b], called puncturable pseudo-random functions (PPRFs). Such a PRF can be evaluated with tha "usual" key k in its full domain, but it is also possible to create so-called punctured keys k_x that allow the evaluation of a PPRF at all points except x, such that its output is indistinguishable from a random value and k_x does not reveal any information about the PRF value at x. As observed concurrently in the publications cited, PPRFs can be realized using the PRF tree of [GGM86]. For a PPRF that is computable in $\mathbf{NC^1}$, see [BLMR13].

2.3 Behind the Scenes of Security Proofs: Assumptions and Security Models

Specifying the security guarantees that a scheme can offer is always a crucial task in cryptography, as the value of a construction is determined by its security. As Silvio Micali noted, "cryptographers seldom sleep well" [Kil88], because even if they do their best and prove that no efficient adversary can break their scheme without solving a problem that is commonly believed to be intractable (e.g. Dlog, DDH, or LWE), their assumption can be shattered the next morning. In this part, we are looking for answers to the following question:

what kind of confidence is provided by the security proofs of current obfuscator candidates and what kinds of uncertainty are still waiting for solutions?

2.3.1 On the "Desirable" and Actual Assumptions behind Obfuscation

Along the way towards building obfuscation, we are going to use both *generic* and *concrete* assumptions. The generic ones assume that a certain cryptographic primitive (e.g. OWF or FHE) exists; this becomes meaningful if the primitive can be instantiated based on a concrete assumption that is a reasonable mathematical conjecture (such as the hardness of factoring). This relation also implies that a generic assumption is better in the sense that it might allow various instantiations, but at the same time it is at most "as good as the concrete assumptions it can be based on" [GK16].

Before discussing the assumptions that are sufficient for building current obfuscators, let us first briefly elaborate on the question *what makes a concrete cryptographic assumption "good"?* First and foremost, it should help in understanding and characterizing of the hardness of breaking a scheme. Naturally, for this, the problem in the assumption should be the subject of previous independent studies, which also requires that the problem is not tied to a given cryptographic primitive, but it is interesting in its own right.[10] We can say that these rather subjective requirements are fulfilled by all standard assumptions, such as Dlog, DDH, and LWE. However, when we are not able to reduce security to any of these "good" assumptions, we have either to leave the standard model by restricting the adversary (see §2.3.2–2.3.4 on this), or to make new assumptions that are necessarily less well understood. In the latter case, it is essential to have objective measures, at least to estimate how well one can sleep after building – in our case – an iO scheme on a new assumption.

A straightforward goal is to avoid the embedding of any structural properties of the scheme into the assumption, thus sweeping aside real challenges. Such a depen-

---

[10] Contrarily, an extreme assumption could even state that a given scheme is secure, but such assumptions do not take us closer to an understanding of the security of the scheme, and thus can be considered inappropriate.

dence between the scheme and the assumption can be hidden in so-called uber- or meta-assumptions that are succinctly formulated collections of (even exponentially many) other assumptions. Such a formulation can also hinder the task of revealing whether the assumption is actually false. This leads us to the problem of falsifiability, an essential property of scientific statements, which was considered for cryptographic assumptions by [Nao03, GW11, Pas13]. Roughly speaking, falsifiability requires that it should be efficiently decidable whether or not an attacker is able to break the assumption.[11] Obviously, without this property, it becomes very hard to position an assumption. Last but not least, it also matters what level of security is required from an assumption. As observed in several publications (see e.g. [GLSW15]), sub-exponential hardness of the assumption seems inherent when iO is based on any instance-independent assumptions.

Next, we review and compare (in Table 2.3) the non-standard assumptions, that have been used to prove the security of iO candidates. Among the generic assumptions, the only non-standard one – in the sense that it is not known to be instantiable from standard concrete assumptions – is the existence of the super-linear stretch PRGs with constant input locality that we discussed in §2.2.5. We now give an intuitive (and informal) description of the concrete assumptions used:

- The bounded speedup hypothesis (BSH) of [BR14a] "is a scaled-down version of the exponential time hypothesis (ETH) [IP99]: whereas the latter asserts that SAT solvers cannot do much better than a brute force search over the space of 2^n solutions, BSH asserts that even solving SAT over smaller solution spaces cannot improve much over brute force search," as the authors of [BR14a] interpret their assumption. [MSW15] proposed an alternative version of the hypothesis (BSH$'$) and also suggested that the original BSH was false.
- The symmetric external Diffie–Hellman assumption (SXDH) [Rot13] in the asymmetric bilinear setting states that the DDH problem is hard in both groups (which is considered to be a standard assumption up to $\kappa = 2$). This naturally extends to more groups as well[12] (which are abstracted by tags in GESs).
- The joint SXDH (jSXDH), proposed by [LV16a], strengthens SXDH by assuming that even the joint distribution of $([a]_{T_i}, [b]_{T_i}, [ab]_{T_i})_{T_i \in \mathbb{T}}$ for a tag universe $\mathbb{T}$ is hard to distinguish from $([a]_{T_i}, [b]_{T_i}, [r]_{T_i})_{T_i \in \mathbb{T}}$, where r is random and a, b are the same for all T_i.
- The multilinear subgroup elimination assumption (MSE) of [GLW14] is the multilinear generalization of the bilinear subgroup decision assumption (SD) assumption of [BGN05], which states that in a composite-order group[13] it is hard to decide whether an element is in a specific subgroup or not.

---

[11] For example, breaking the factoring assumption can be efficiently checked given the claimed prime factors; at the same time, the assumption that an obfuscator fulfils the definition of iO is not falsifiable, as it cannot be decided efficiently whether two circuits indeed compute the same function.

[12] When considering GESs, instead of MMaps, the caveat is that the groups considered should not be "pairable", either directly or indirectly, as that would trivially refute the assumption.

[13] Without knowing the factorization of the group order.

Table 2.3: Comparison of the non-standard assumptions made about GESs and MMaps.

Property/assumption	EPI	SSGES	SSGES'	MSE	GGHZ	AS	jSXDH	SXDH
Efficiently falsifiable	×	×	✓	✓	✓	✓	✓	✓
Instance-independent	×	×	✓	✓	✓	✓	✓	✓
No sub-exponential hardness needed	✓	✓	×	×	×	×	×	×
Plausible with current GESs	×	×	×	×	×	(?)	×	×
Prime or composite-order needed	p	p	p	c	c	p	p	p
Constant degree is enough	×	×	×	×	×	✓	✓	✓

- The GGHZ assumption of [GGHZ16] consists of two subgroup decision assumptions, so in spirit it is close to the MSE assumption.
- The semantic security of GESs (SSGES), formulated by [PST14], assumes roughly speaking that encodings of two elements (of a ring) under the same tag are indistinguishable even in the presence of encodings of "auxiliary" elements under different tags, as long as the encoded values are sampled from a "valid" distribution, meaning that they do not leak information to a generic attacker (see §2.3.2 for more about such attackers). A closer look shows that SSGES is an (exponential-size) collection of assumptions, one for each valid distribution. As a potential proof may rely on instances of the assumption that depend on the scheme, SSGES is instance-dependent and non-falsifiable, as checking the validity of a distribution might not be efficient. [PST14] also considered a variant of the assumption, SSGES', that eliminates the above drawbacks while requiring sub-exponential hardness. Other variants were proposed in [BCKP14, Lin16].
- The AS assumptions of [AS17, §7.2.1] are two rather ad hoc, non-succinct assumptions about prime-order GESs. In turn, they are conjectured to be instantiable using current GES candidates, as no low-level encodings of 0 are required to be given out. This is justified in the BGKPS model (see §2.3.4).
- The equivalent program indistinguishability (EPI) assumption considers a specific transformation T of MBPs and states roughly that "if for two different ways of fixing some inputs to an MBP result in the same function on the remaining non-fixed inputs, then it is infeasible to decide which of the two sets of fixed inputs is used in a given output of T" [GGH+13b]. This is justified in the GCMM model (see §2.3.4).

2.3.2 The Idea of Ideal Models

As the necessary assumptions are not known to be plausible for current GES candidates, we need different tools to argue security. The common way of facilitating proofs is via idealizing the adversary. In other words, one can separate attacks based on the properties utilized, and assume that an adversary cannot make use of certain properties. In this way, it is enough to prove security against the corresponding restricted adversaries. For instance, the widely used random oracle model (ROM) [BR93] considers ideal adversaries that interact with a "random oracle" instead of evaluating a concrete hash function. This separates attacks on a concrete scheme, by neglecting the ones that utilize the weaknesses of hash functions.

This form of idealization both gives a persuasive intuition about security and helps to better understand the nature of the weaknesses that are still possible, because these must be caused by differences between the imagined and the real attacker. The idea behind the ideal models proposed for the security analysis of obfuscator candidates originates from the generic group model (GGM) of [Nec94, Sho97, Mau05] for elliptic-curve-group-based cryptosystems. The main assumption of the GGM is that any attack is independent of the specific structure of the group in which a scheme is instantiated. The model captures such generic attacks by substituting the concrete elements and operation with access to a "group oracle" that has two tasks. It can be queried for group elements, and for any i it answers (consistently) with a generic representation $\sigma(i)$, called a "handle", that is a random bit string (instead of $g^i \in G$ in any specific group). In order to execute the group operation, the oracle also has to be queried, and it replies with the handle of the output if the input handles are valid. The so-called ideal GES (or MMap) models, in which many obfuscator candidates have been analysed, are generalizations of the GGM that build on similar restrictions on the adversary. Namely, the oracle implements the intended functionality of a GES (introduced in §2.2.4), allowing the evaluation of polynomials of a predetermined degree, as opposed to the linear operations in the GGM.

2.3.3 Idealizations vs Reality: Criticism and Interpretations

Before going into details of the different flavours of idealization, we have to elaborate on the criticism of these models. It has been shown that there exist (rather contrived) schemes that are provably secure in the ROM or in the GGM, but for which any implementation of the oracle leads to insecure schemes in the standard model (see [CGH04] and [Den02], respectively). Note, however, that this does not mean that a security proof in these models entails real-world vulnerabilities [KM07, KM15]. Unfortunately, investigating the security of obfuscation in these models is even more intricate.

Obfuscation in the ROM was first considered by [LPS04], who showed positive results for specific functionalities. General-purpose VBB and iO obfuscation, however, were ruled out in the ROM in the general setting, where each entity (the obfuscator and also its input and output programs) has access to the oracle [BGI+01, GR07]. [CKP15] extended[14] the VBB impossibility to the case where the program to be obfuscated is fully specified, i.e. cannot make oracle queries.

---

[14] Assuming trapdoor permutations exist.

[PS16, MMN16] showed that the generalization of the GGM still provides enough power to an adversary to break VBB obfuscation of certain functionalities when the oracle allows the evaluation of any *constant*-degree polynomial. At the same time, the state of affairs changes dramatically when the allowed degree is not a constant any more but can depend, for example on the input to the obfuscator. For ideal GES models, the VBB impossibility result of [BGI+01] does not apply, as the counterexample of those authors requires an explicit and succinct representation of the obfuscated programs (see §3.1.1) that is infeasible if a program contains calls to a non-succinct oracle. Indeed, several obfuscator constructions are provably VBB secure (see Table 5.1) in ideal GES models, while we know that in the standard model VBB obfuscation is impossible in general, indicating that these idealizations of GESs fail to capture attacks that are possible in real life.

How can one interpret security analyses of obfuscators in such models in light of the contradiction with impossibility results in the standard model? We list several interpretations in the following, from pessimistic to sanguine:

- Any proof of VBB security in an ideal GES model can be viewed as a criticism of that model as it fails to capture real attacks.
- Such a proof demonstrates resistance against a wide class of generic attacks but does not say anything about techniques that make use of the inner structure of the GES.
- The model can be realized by implementing a GES on (stateless) secure hardware, which is enough to obtain VBB obfuscation of any program on that specific hardware.
- Refinement of ideal models (together with security proofs) can help us to better understand the security properties of candidate obfuscators and the nature of VBB impossibility as the possible attacks must rely on specific properties, and the interesting properties of any unobfuscatable functionalities need to be such that they cannot be captured by the ideal models (e.g. the "self-eating" property discussed in §3.1.3). In this way, working on arguments in these models may result in better relaxations of obfuscation security or open the way to basing obfuscation on standard cryptographic assumptions.

2.3.4 Variants of Ideal GES Models

We close our review of ideal models by summarizing the deviations of the proposed GES oracle variants from each other. The importance of these rather small differences lies in their influence on the power given to an adversary. We focus on those models which have been used to analyse general-purpose obfuscator candidates and have a candidate instantiation as well[15] (see §2.2.4).

---

[15] That is why neither the black-box group model over pseudo-free groups of [CV13] nor the weak ideal GES model of [BMSZ16] is presented here(the abstract structure and thus the obfuscator

The common property of all ideal GES models, as discussed above, is that in order to represent an encoding $[a_i]_{T_i}$ of a_i with tag T_i, the oracle gives out a handle h_i that explicitly specifies T_i but is independent of a_i. The handles can only be used for further operation queries to the oracle, which are answered according to the functionality of the modelled GES. Note that obfuscation requires a secret-key GES, and thus encoding queries are available only to the obfuscator, while the adversary can make operation queries using the available handles. The current models are characterized by the following properties of the oracle.

Representation of Encodings. In current GES candidates, encodings are randomized (§2.2.4) such that the oracle can model them by giving out a new random handle as its response to any query, regardless of the value of the encoding that the handle substitutes for. In order to be able to answer operation queries, the oracle has to maintain a list of assignments $h_i \rightarrow a_i$ that it can look up. This kind of *multiple-representation* model was first used in [BGK+14]. Simplifying the oracle to always represent the same value with a *single* handle helps the adversary (as the adversary can see equivalences without the aid of the oracle) and thus leads to a less restrictive model, which was first used by [BR13].

Restrictions on Operations. While ideally a GES supports only operations on inputs with the proper tags, we might assume that an adversary is able to sidestep this restriction:

Addition/subtraction. As observed by [MSW15], the [GGH13a, CLT13] GES candidates permit additions of incompatible encodings, motivating the relaxation of the rules of addition in ideal models. Their oracle answers addition queries regardless of the tags of the inputs, while in other, more restricted models the oracle does not reply if the tags are not compatible.

Multiplication. Multiplication of encodings with incompatible tags is not known to be computable currently. Nevertheless, [MSW15] considered a model with unrestricted multiplication in order to broaden the classes of attacks captured by the ideal model.

Zero-testing. Similarly to the previous operations, zero-testing also can be captured by the model, with or without the restriction on tag compatibility.

[PS16] proposed a generalized way of handling operations: the only operation is a polynomial evaluation over the initial handles that returns the result 0 or 1 as long as a "legality predicate" that can capture all of the above restrictions accepts the requested polynomial.

Representation of Zero-Test Output. Ideally, the zero-testing operation outputs a single bit. In fact, in current GES constructions, the output is an element of a ring R (just like a_i), based on which the bit can be determined (if it is "small", the output

---

construction of the former have no candidate instantiation, while the latter was considered only for the analysis of a special-purpose obfuscator).

Table 2.4: Variants of idealized models.

Property/idealized model	GCMM[18]	BR	BGKPS	MSW-1	MSW-2	MSZ	GMM+
Multiple (m) or unique (u) representation	u	u	m	m	m	m	m
Unrestricted multiplication	×	×	×	×	✓	×	×
Unrestricted addition	×	×	×	✓	✓	×	×
Unrestricted zero-test	–	×	×	✓	✓	×	×
Successful zero-test output is 1 or a handle (h)	–	1	1	1	1	h	h

is 1, and 0 otherwise). This property serves as the basis of several attacks (see §5.3) which fall outside of the scope of models that represent the output of this operation with a single bit. [CGH$^+$15, Appendix A] and [MSZ16] devised the first model in which this is not the case. In the case of a successful zero-test, instead of returning 1, the oracle answers with a handle to a ring element that can be used later on. This more precise model builds not on the expected functionality of a GES but on its concrete implementation details, narrowing the gap between the real and the ideal attack environment. Without going into details of the relations with GES candidates, we give a high-level description[16] of the behaviour of the generalized oracle.

Let f_i denote formal polynomials over $\mathbb{Z}_p$, and g, r_i formal variables (for all i and for a prime p). On an encoding query for $[a_i]_{T_i}$, the oracle picks a random r_i and defines $f_i := a_i + r_i \cdot g$ besides generating the handle h_i (which explicitly determines the tag T_i but is independent of a_i), and stores $h_i \to f_i$. On an operation query $\circ \in \{+, -, \cdot\}$ for h_i, h_j (with compatible tags), the oracle returns (and stores) a handle for $f = f_i \circ f_j$ with the corresponding tag. When zero-testing h_i, the oracle checks whether the constant term of the corresponding f_i is zero. If not, it returns 0, otherwise f_i must be divisible by g, so a handle h_i' is given out for $f_i' := f_i/g$ and stored together in a "post-zero-test list". Possible manipulations of the zero-test outputs are captured by a special opportunity for a query to the oracle. On an m-variate polynomial $Q(h_1', \ldots, h_m')$ of post-zero-test handles, the oracle checks if $Q(f_1', \ldots, f_m')$ is zero modulo g but non-zero as a polynomial over $\mathbb{Z}_p$, and outputs a "win" flag if yes and $\perp$ otherwise. We note that the ability to gain a win flag[17] is necessary to mount the attacks that we discuss in §5.3. Another, more general variant of this model was proposed by [GMM$^+$16], in which r_i is not an independent formal variable but might depend on all a_i.

A summary of current ideal GES models and their properties is given in Table 2.4.

---

[16] For a precise description of the model, we refer to [GMM$^+$16, §2].

[17] In fact, to find a non-trivial element in the ideal $\langle g \rangle$.

[18] In contrast to the rest of the models, the GCMM considers "ordered" matrices behind the handles, and the restrictions on the operations are determined based on this order, which is specified by assigning left and right colours to each matrix (addition is possible in the case of matching colours, while multiplication is allowed when the right colour of the first matrix matches the left colour of the other).

Chapter 3
Definitional Approaches

Before reviewing the state of the art in building cryptographic obfuscators, we need to clarify first the goals of this primitive, especially as, in contrast to the "code obfuscation" techniques in daily use, we are seeking to fulfil precise security guarantees. As we are going to see, capturing the intuitive goals of obfuscation in formal definitions turns out to be rather tricky. Informally speaking, we expect three properties from an obfuscator $\mathcal{O}$ that takes as input a circuit C and outputs another circuit $\mathcal{O}[C]$. First, $\mathcal{O}[C]$ should preserve the original functionality of C. Second, the size (representing efficiency) of $\mathcal{O}[C]$ should remain comparable to the size of C. And third, we expect that $\mathcal{O}[C]$ should be in some sense "unintelligible" to anyone, even those who run it. While the first two requirements are fairly straightforward to formulate, the "unintelligibility" property is more challenging and can be captured in various ways.

The investigation of the right definition of obfuscation was initiated by Hada [Had00] and soon afterwards the seminal work of Barak et al. [BGI^{+}01, BGI^{+}12] drew attention to the problem of finding the proper formulation. In this section, we investigate the following questions:

What do we expect from an obfuscator, and how can we formalize this?
Which of the current definitions seem to be viable and which are known to be impossible to realize?
What kinds of relaxation of the requirements are meaningful, and what is the relationship between the different definitional approaches?

3.1 Security via Simulation

3.1.1 Virtual Black-Box Obfuscation

The strongest theoretical notion of obfuscation security requires an obfuscated circuit to leak at most as much information as already leaked by the circuit's input–

© The Author(s), under exclusive licence to Springer Nature Switzerland AG 2020   29
M. Horváth and L. Buttyán, *Cryptographic Obfuscation*, SpringerBriefs
in Computer Science, https://doi.org/10.1007/978-3-319-98041-6_3

output behaviour. In other words, the obfuscated circuit should behave like a "virtual black box" (hence the name), i.e. anything that can be computed from it (including also its description) must be computable merely from its input–output pairs. From a cryptographic perspective, the view of an attacker $\mathcal{A}$ (in practice any user) of an obfuscated circuit $\mathcal{O}[C]$ is required to be indistinguishable from a simulator $\mathcal{S}^C$ with merely oracle access to the circuit.

Definition 3.1 (VBB obfuscation [BGI+01]).

A PPT algorithm $\mathcal{O}$ that takes as input a circuit C from a circuit family $\mathcal{C} = \{\mathcal{C}_n\}_{n\in\mathbb{N}}$ of polynomial-size circuits with input length n and outputs a new circuit $\mathcal{O}[C]$ is said to be a virtual black-box obfuscator for that family if it has the following properties:

- *Functionality-preserving:* For every circuit C, $\mathcal{O}[C]$ describes a circuit that computes the same function as C.
- *Polynomial slowdown:* There exists a polynomial poly, such that for every circuit $C, |\mathcal{O}[C]| \le \text{poly}(|C|)$.
- *Virtual black-box:* For any PPT adversary $\mathcal{A}$, there exists a PPT simulator $\mathcal{S}$ and a negligible function $\text{neg}(n)$ such that for every input length n and every $C \in \mathcal{C}_n$,

$$|\Pr[\mathcal{A}(\mathcal{O}[C]) = 1] - \Pr[\mathcal{S}^C(1^n) = 1]| \le \text{neg}(n),$$

where the probability is taken over the coins of the adversary, the simulator, and the obfuscator.

3.1.2 Variants of the VBB Paradigm

We mention here some possible alterations of the above definition. The constraint about functionality is often used in a slightly weaker form which allows the functionalities of C and $\mathcal{O}[C]$ to differ with negligible probability. A possible strengthening of the VBB property is inspired by the experience that, most probably, a real-life adversary will have some a priori information about the obfuscated program being examined. This expectation was captured in [GK05] by providing both $\mathcal{A}$ and $\mathcal{S}$ with an auxiliary input, which either is allowed to depend on C or must be independent of it. The latter clearly leads to a weaker notion, although this is still stronger than Definition 3.1 (which corresponds to the case of an empty auxiliary input).

Also, note that the VBB property above defined requires indistinguishability for all possible input circuits to the obfuscator even in the worst case. [GK05] relaxes this requirement by also accepting if $\mathcal{A}$ and $\mathcal{S}$ are indistinguishable for a circuit C randomly chosen from $\mathcal{C}$, or, in other words, if $\mathcal{A}$ and $\mathcal{S}$ are indistinguishable on average. Intuitively, if we consider "worst-case" VBB obfuscation with an auxiliary input, security requires indistinguishability for all possible combinations of circuits and auxiliary information, while for "average-case" VBB it is enough that indistinguishability holds for a random circuit.

3.1.3 Evidence of VBB Impossibility

While Definition 3.1 seems to capture the intuitive goal quite naturally, the seminal work of [BGI+01] showed that we cannot hope to realize it in general. A little more precisely, assuming the existence of OWFs,[1] the authors of [BGI+01] managed to show a circuit family that is strongly not learnable but, given *any* description of the functionality, included obfuscated ones, can be efficiently reverse-engineered. To grasp the idea behind unobfuscatable functions (in the VBB sense), imagine a program $P_{\alpha,\beta}(x)$ that returns a secret value β if and only if $x = \alpha$ and outputs 0 otherwise. Let this simple password-checking-like algorithm be a subroutine of $P'_{\alpha,\beta}(b,x)$ that runs it on x if the binary input b is 0. When $b = 1$, P' interprets x as a program description and runs it for a predetermined number of steps (e.g. on input α) to decide whether it is equivalent to $P_{\alpha,\beta}$, and outputs β if so and 0 otherwise. This contrived program is indeed not learnable, as if one has merely black-box access to P' the probability of finding the secret β (or a non-zero output) is negligible (for an appropriate domain size). At the same time, given any description of P', even a VBB-obfuscated one, it is enough to feed the program to itself, i.e. to compute $P'_{\alpha,\beta}(1,P'_{\alpha,\beta}(0,\cdot))$, in order to reveal the secret β.

Later, the above negative result was strengthened in several ways. [GK05] also ruled out the weaker, average-case VBB notion (with respect to the auxiliary input[2]) without further assumptions. Assuming the existence of trapdoor permutations, [BP13] extended the negative result to "approximate" VBB obfuscators that do not preserve the circuit's functionality for all inputs, but only for most of them. Several other impossibility results were shown in models other than the standard model, such as in the ROM by [CKP15] (also assuming trapdoor permutations) and in further idealized models (see §2.3.2) by [PS16, MMN16].

It is worth noting that Definition 3.1 requires only the existence of the corresponding simulator S for a given A, but it does not say anything about how hard it is to find S. [BCC+14] avoided this weakness by requiring the existence of an efficient transformation from an adversary to the corresponding simulator or, equivalently, the existence of a universal PPT S that is capable of simulating any PPT A. Somewhat counter-intuitively, these authors showed that VBB obfuscation with a universal simulator is also impossible for certain function families[3] if iO, a weaker notion of obfuscation (see §3.2.1), is possible in general. Regarding the perspects for quantum computing, [Aar05] asked whether quantum black-box obfuscation is impossible as well. The answer seems yes, according to [AF16], where different flavours of quantum VBB obfuscation were shown to be impossible to realize.

These results rule out the possibility of constructing a *general-purpose* obfuscator in the VBB sense by showing some specific unobfuscatable circuit families,

---

[1] In the case of Turing machine (Glossary)s, even this assumption is unnecessary.

[2] Note that worst-case VBB obfuscation with an auxiliary input is stronger than Definition 3.1, so the negative result of [BGI+01] extends to it.

[3] For function families $\mathcal{F}$ with super-polynomial pseudo-entropy that include, for example, PRFs or semantically secure PKE. Informally, in such an $\mathcal{F}$ it is hard to detect if a function has been modified in some random locations.

although other interesting program families might still be VBB obfuscatable even if currently we are not able to determine them. This leads to one possible line of research into ways ways of avoiding the negative results.

Despite the impossibility of the VBB notion, this characterization of the "unintelligibility" property gives an intuition about how obfuscation could be used to solve long-standing open problems in cryptography (e.g. how to turn a symmetric-key encryption scheme into a public-key one). This raises the hope that by relaxing the security requirement of obfuscation – such that it still remains meaningful, but bypasses the negative results – we can get a notion which can substitute for the use of VBB obfuscators with some effort. In the remainder of this section, we summarize the results obtained along the path to finding such a weaker definition.

3.1.4 Virtual Grey-Box Obfuscation

The virtual grey-box (VGB) notion was coined by Bitansky and Canetti [BC14] and it weakens the black-box property by increasing the capabilities of the simulator. Instead of a PPT simulator, the VGB property allows S to use unbounded computational time while still permitting only polynomially many queries to the oracle.

Although the VGB is clearly a relaxation of the VBB (since a PPT simulator for VBB security satisfies VGB security as well, but not vice versa), the counterexample of [BGI+01] also rules out this weaker notion when TMs are considered. At the same time, currently we do not know of any such negative results for circuits; moreover, there is a candidate VGB obfuscator for circuits [BCKP14], suggesting that this notion might be realizable.

We mention that the modifications that we presented for the VBB requirements remain meaningful for the VGB model as well. Interestingly, [BC14] showed that the notions of worst-case VGB obfuscation with and without auxiliary information are equivalent.

3.2 Indistinguishability-Based Security

3.2.1 Indistinguishability Obfuscation

The approaches above compared obfuscated programs with theoretical constructs called "black boxes". In fact, our goal in obfuscation is to transform programs to a form that is "more secure" than others. A natural way to verify the success of such transformations is to compare their output with other programs. This concept appears in the following formulations of "unintelligibility".

Besides negative results, [BGI+01] also suggested two weaker definitions that avoid the VBB paradigm but still lead to meaningful and precise notions of obfus-

Fig. 3.1: Notions of efficient obfuscation and their (known) implications.

cation security. These definitions, i.e. indistinguishability obfuscation and differing-input obfuscation (iO and DiO for short), require that if two circuits of similar size compute the same function, then their obfuscations should be indistinguishable.

Definition 3.2 (iO [BGI⁺01]). An indistinguishability obfuscator is defined by the functionality-preserving and slowdown requirements of Definition 3.1, while the virtual black-box property is replaced with the following:

- *Indistinguishability:* for any PPT $\mathcal{A}$, there is a negligible function neg such that, for any two circuits C_1 and C_2 that compute the same function and are of the same size n, it holds that

$$|\Pr[\mathcal{A}(\mathcal{O}(C_1)) = 1] - \Pr[\mathcal{A}(\mathcal{O}(C_2)) = 1]| \le \operatorname{neg}(n).$$

As we have already seen in the Introduction, the iO requirement is realizable, at least inefficiently. An interesting consequence of Example 1.1 is that if **P=NP** (which is the case in "Algorithmica", the imaginary world of Impagliazzo [Imp95]), then iO obfuscation exists while the rest of cryptography can be considered dead. This fact shows that iO alone does not imply hardness. Therefore, in applications it is always used together with other primitives for example with OWFs.

3.2.2 Different Faces of iO

The Best-Possible Obfuscation. Example 1.1 also raises the question of whether iO obfuscation hides any information. [GR07] managed to overcome the limitation that the definition lacks an intuitive security guarantee by showing that an *efficient* iO obfuscator achieves the maximum we can hope for in terms of hiding information in a program. The authors of [GR07] defined best-possible obfuscation (BPO), arguing that if any information exposed by $\mathcal{O}[C]$ is also exposed by every other functionally equivalent circuit of similar size, then $\mathcal{O}[C]$ is the best-possible obfuscation. Although this definition allows $\mathcal{O}[C]$ to leak non-black-box information when VBB obfuscation is not possible, the best-possible obfuscation is essentially VBB secure whenever this is achievable (otherwise the VBB obfuscation of the same circuit would leak less information than the obfuscation examined, contradicting the

requirement that it is "best-possible"). As we have already hinted, [GR07] proved
that iO and BPO are equivalent for efficient obfuscators. The intuition behind the
equivalence is the following. Suppose that, for a concrete circuit C, there exists some
strong form of obfuscation, for example VBB. Take two instances of C, obfuscate
one of them using $\mathcal{O}_{VBB}$, and pad the other one to a size $|\mathcal{O}_{VBB}[C]|$. By iO obfus-
cating the resulting (functionally equivalent) circuits, we get two indistinguishable
circuits:

$$\mathcal{O}_{iO}[\mathcal{O}_{VBB}[C]] \sim \mathcal{O}_{iO}[\text{Pad}[C]].$$

As VBB security must hold after any further transformations, the circuit on the left-
hand side should not leak more information than $\mathcal{O}_{VBB}[C]$ does, but, according to
the definition of iO, even $\mathcal{O}_{iO}[\text{Pad}[C]]$ cannot reveal more, because otherwise we
could distinguish it from $\mathcal{O}_{iO}[\mathcal{O}_{VBB}[C]]$. It follows that $\mathcal{O}_{iO}$ alone must be as secure
as $\mathcal{O}_{VBB}$.

     With this, the technically easier-to-use iO notion can be applied with the strong
intuitive security guarantee of the "best-possible" definition implying that if a functionality is VBB obfuscatable, then *any* iO obfuscator for this functionality is VBB
secure.

Relation between Simulation- and Indistinguishability-Based Definitions.   In
[BR14b] the authors gave a surprising alternative form of Definition 3.2, formulated
in the language of VBB and VGB notions, pointing out connections between the
different ideas (see Fig. 3.1 for a summary). As it turns out, iO is equivalent to a
relaxation of VGB obfuscation, where the computationally unbounded simulator is
allowed to make an unbounded number of queries to the oracle (see the proof of
[BR14b, Lemma 2.9]). In other words, the efficiency of simulation is the crucial
property that differentiates VBB, VGB, and iO.

     A different aspect of the same relationship is captured through the notion of
strong iO (SiO), proposed by [BCKP14]. Informally, an obfuscator is said to provide
SiO if the indistinguishability of obfuscations holds for circuits C and C' that are
taken from a distribution where the probability of $C(x) \neq C'(x)$ is negligible for all
x. [BCKP14] proved that SiO is in the end equivalent to VGB obfuscation, i.e. SiO
is the formulation of VGB obfuscation in the language of iO.

     Later on, we are going to focus on the first iO candidate, presented by Garg et al.
[GGH+13b], and review further research that was motivated by their work.

3.2.3 Relaxing the Efficiency Requirement: XiO

Recall that the efficiency of iO requires that both the running time of the obfuscation algorithm and the size of the resulting circuit have to be polynomial in the
size of the input circuit C. These conditions stand in contrast to the trivial solution
(which exists unconditionally [BGI+01]) that is to compute C for all n inputs and
output its function table, requiring $\text{poly}(|C|) \cdot 2^n$ time and size. [LPST16a] proposed

a relaxed notion of efficiency in between these two extremes. In terms of obfuscated program size, so-called exponentially efficient iO (XiO) requires only slightly better performance than preparing the truth table, namely $|\mathcal{O}_{\text{XiO}}[C]| < \text{poly}(|C|) \cdot 2^{\varepsilon n}$ has to hold for some $\varepsilon > 0$, while the obfuscation time does not have to be better than trivial. If the time satisfies the same bound as the size, the obfuscator is said to be a strong XiO (SXiO) [BNPW16]. While being so close to the brute-force method may look meaningless at first sight, XiO turns out to be surprisingly powerful (see §4.4.3). Nevertheless, note that as a result of its "lazy" approach, the use of XiO makes sense only for circuits with logarithmic input length (either in the security parameter or in the circuit size).

Later on, when we refer to SXiO, it is always meant that the compression factor ε can be "sufficiently small", and the notation SXiO' denotes that ε is only "slightly smaller" than 1 (i.e. SXiO' is less efficient).

3.2.4 Differing-Input or Extractability Obfuscation

An Intuition.   A stronger form of iO, differing-input obfuscation (DiO), a.k.a extractibility obfuscation, was also proposed by [BGI+01]. Informally speaking, DiO guarantees that if an adversary $\mathcal{A}$ can distinguish between obfuscations $\mathcal{O}_{\text{DiO}}[C]$, and $\mathcal{O}_{\text{DiO}}(C')$ of two circuits C and C', then $\mathcal{A}$ must also be able to efficiently recover a point x on which C and C' differ, i.e. $C(x) \neq C'(x)$ (or, in other words, such an x *must be efficiently extractable from* $\mathcal{A}$).

For an example of circuits for which it is hard to find differing inputs, imagine two signature verification circuits of a signature scheme with different verification keys hard-coded into them. According to the unforgeability property of the signature scheme, it is hard to find a valid message–signature pair that is accepted by one of the verification circuits, i.e. an input on which the circuits have different outputs (as otherwise both of them reject). In this way, the DiO obfuscations of these functionally non-equivalent circuits have to be indistinguishable according to the definition. On the flip side, if C and C' are functionally equivalent, then no differing input exists, and thus the DiO requirement coincides with that of iO.

Impossibilities and Relaxations.   Intuitively, the DiO notion seems to be only slightly stronger than iO; however, [GGHW14] showed that under the assumption that a given special-purpose obfuscation exists, general-purpose DiO with general auxiliary input cannot exist. Using this result, [BP15] ruled out DiO in the absence of auxiliary input. [BSW16] gave evidence against the existence of DiO for TMs assuming the existence of either OWFs or iO.

On the positive side, [BCP14] demonstrated that iO directly implies a weak form of the differing-input notion, in which extraction of the input is required only when the pair of circuits differ on only polynomially[4] many inputs. [IPS15] proposed a weaker DiO variant, called public-coin DiO, that requires the auxiliary input to be a public random string (containing the randomness used in sampling C and C'). While this definition still allows useful applications of DiO, it avoids the previous negative results. However, our confidence in this weaker definition is undermined by [BP15], which showed contradictions between the existence of public-coin DiO and so-called "knowledge assumptions" in certain circumstances. Finally, we should mention the framework of [BST14], which aims to capture different notions of iO and DiO in a comparable way and also helps one to define weaker, but still realizable, DiO variants by altering the requirements on the auxiliary input.

---

[4] Polynomial in the security parameter.

Chapter 4
Bootstrapping: From the Seed to the Flower

The key question that bootstrapping seeks to answer is the following:

what is the simplest object that we can to transform into a general-purpose obfuscator using standard cryptographic assumptions?

In this section, we are going to investigate bootstrapping solutions that amplify different primitives to achieve iO for all polynomial-size circuits. More concretely, the starting point of these transformations is either obfuscation for some specific circuit classes (§4.1–4.2) or various forms of functional encryption (§4.3–4.4).

Note that building obfuscators for arbitrary functions with the help of a limited obfuscator is an intriguing problem even if we do not have proper algorithms for the limited task,[1] because it could also be implemented using tamper-proof hardware. This possibility was investigated by [GO96, And08], relying on hardware that is able to maintain state, and [GIS+10, §6.2], who showed that stateless hardware also suffices.[2] [BCG+11] gave a general transformation obtained from these methods to enable the use of leaky hardware as well.

Nevertheless, in this section, we are not interested in the realization of these bootstrappable objects and focus only on the bootstrapping techniques themselves. At the same time, we consider only transformations the starting point of which have candidate realizations without assuming special hardware (we discuss these candidates in §5–6). While bootstrapping is aimed at using standard assumptions such as LWE or the existence of PKE, identity-based encryption (IBE), RE, or FHE, when focusing on FE-based solutions, we are also going to deal with "unorthodox" bootstrapping methods (in §4.4.3) that use non-standard assumptions, such as that super-linear stretch PRGs exist in $\mathbf{NC}^0$ (about the feasibility of these assumptions, see §2.2.5). The benefit of this more permissive attitude is that it can help to reduce

---

[1] At the time of writing, we do not have secure core-obfuscators based on well-studied cryptographic assumptions.

[2] At a high level, the method relies on tamper-proof hardware for the evaluation of the gates of an encrypted circuit: it first decrypts the input wires, evaluates the gate, and then encrypts the result. Note that in some idealized models, the tamper-proof hardware can be substituted by a VBB obfuscator for the required functionality.

© The Author(s), under exclusive licence to Springer Nature Switzerland AG 2020

M. Horváth and L. Buttyán, *Cryptographic Obfuscation*, SpringerBriefs
in Computer Science, https://doi.org/10.1007/978-3-319-98041-6_4

the complexity of the starting FE scheme, which will only have to work for simple functions such as constant-degree polynomials.

A summary of bootstrapping methods, independent of FE, is given in Table 4.1, and an overview of all transformations is depicted in Fig. 4.1.

Table 4.1: Summary of bootstrapping methods that amplify obfuscators for circuits from a complexity class WEAK to obfuscation for **P/poly** for different notions of obfuscation. * denotes that the circuit size of the functionality which is required to be obfuscated using some core-obfuscator is independent of the size of the circuit that we actually want to obfuscate.

Proposed by	Achieved notion	Class WEAK	Applied tools	Functionality to be obfuscated
[GIS+10]	VBB	NC^1	Symmetric key encryption	Symmetric key encryption and decryption*
[GGH+13b]	iO, VBB	NC^1	FHE, NIWI	NIWI verification, FHE decryption
[BCP14, ABG+13]	DiO	NC^1	FHE, SNARK	SNARK verification, FHE decryption
[App14a]	VBB	TC^0	RE, PRF	RE encoding
[CLTV15]	iO	NC^1	RE, PPRF	RE encoding
[BGL+15]	iO	NC^1	pdRE	pdRE encoding*
[BISW17]	VBB	NC^1	FHE, SNARG	SNARG verification, FHE decryption*

4.1 Amplifying Obfuscation with the Help of FHE

In §1.2 and §2.2.1, we have already touched upon the common property of FHE and obfuscation, namely that both hide information about function evaluation. The idea of using FHE for the goals of obfuscation appeared in [BCG+11], but [GGH+13b] showed first how to use this technique in the case of iO. In this part, we are going to introduce these ideas, initially assuming that we have access to a VBB obfuscator for NC^1 circuits and then showing how to relax this assumption and bootstrap iO for NC^1 circuits.

4.1.1 Bootstrapping VBB Obfuscation

Let us recall first the main differences between FHE and obfuscation. While the homomorphic evaluation function works over the ciphertext space, obfuscation has ordinary plaintext inputs and outputs. Moreover, FHE does not have any guarantees of the secrecy of the evaluated function. The first problem can be solved after observing that the decryption circuits of most FHE schemes (e.g. [Gen09, GSW13]) are in NC^1, and hence the circuit can be obfuscated even with a restricted obfuscator that works only for low-depth circuits. Think of the following (at this point still

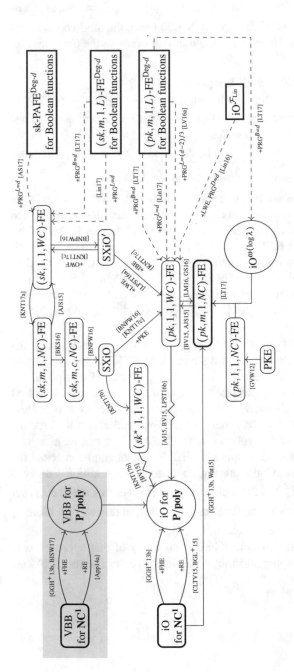

Fig. 4.1: Bootstrapping theorems for obfuscation. The frames around the primitives indicate the complexity class of functions that they can handle (circles denote **P/poly**, rounded rectangles correspond to **NC¹**, and rectangles represent **NC⁰** or, more precisely, constant-degree polynomials). Primitives in bold frames have candidate realizations for which obfuscators for **NC¹** are discussed in §5, while the others are introduced in §6. The grey area is known to be impossible in the standard model, and dashed arrows indicate transformations that are possible using non-standard assumptions. Zigzag arrows indicate that the transformation incurs a sub-exponential security loss.[3] For our notations for FE and PRG schemes, see §2.2.2 and §2.2.5.

---

[3] We note that the transformation of [BKS16] from FE for single-input functions to multi-input functions incurs exponential security loss; however, when it is enough to obtain FE for functions with a constant number of inputs (which is actually the case), this loss remains polynomial, and for this reason the corresponding arrow is not marked with a zigzag.

flawed) bootstrapping idea: let the obfuscation of an arbitrary circuit C consist of an FHE public key PK, an evaluation function $FHE.Eval_{C,PK}(\cdot)$ of C, and the obfuscation $\mathcal{O}_{VBB}^{NC^1}[FHE.Dec_{SK}]$ of the FHE decryption function with the hard-coded secret key SK (corresponding to PK). Having these, a user can evaluate the obfuscated C for input x in three steps:

1. Encrypt x using the given PK as $FHE.Enc(PK,x) = CT_x^{PK}$.
2. Now run the evaluation algorithm on this ciphertext, $FHE.Eval_{C,PK}(CT_x^{PK}) = CT_y^{PK}$, which gives the encrypted result of the computation according to the homomorphic property, meaning that $y = C(x)$.
3. Finally, the resulting ciphertext CT_y^{PK} can be decrypted by evaluating the obfuscated decryption circuit $\mathcal{O}_{VBB}^{NC^1}[FHE.Dec_{SK}](CT_y^{PK}) = y = C(x)$.

This idea clearly solves the input–output problem; however, the secrecy of C is still not maintained, as FHE guarantees only that *data* remains hidden during the computation, and not the evaluated circuit itself. This problem can be solved by invoking universal circuits (see §2.1.1) to transform the program into data as well. When we rethink the previous bootstrapping attempt by using UCs, we need to supplement the obfuscation with $CT_{C'}^{PK} = FHE.Enc(PK,C')$, where C' is the binary description of C. The evaluation function now needs to evaluate a universal circuit U on the encrypted C' and x, $FHE.Eval_{U,PK}(CT_{C'}^{PK}, CT_x^{PK}) = CT_y^{PK}$, in this way hiding the evaluated circuit.[4].

The astute reader might still see a serious flaw in the above construction. Indeed, a user of the obfuscated program could simply feed $CT_{C'}^{PK}$ to the obfuscated decryption circuit, which would output C', making all previous efforts pointless. In order to fill this gap, [GGH+13b] proposed the use of non-interactive (so-called witness-indistinguishable) proof systems. At a high level, the user has to provide a proof π of the honest evaluation of the function FHE.Eval and attach it to the input of an obfuscated *conditional* decryption circuit $FHE.Dec^*$. π can be imagined as a concatenation of the internal wire values of FHE.Eval that can be checked for consistency by a shallow circuit. Consequently, an obfuscated conditional decryption $\mathcal{O}_{VBB}^{NC^1}[FHE.Dec_{SK}^*](\pi, CT_y^{PK})$ can be prepared that first verifies π and decrypts only if CT_y^{PK} is indeed the output of the function FHE.Eval, in this way prohibiting the decryption of *arbitrary* ciphertext, especially $CT_{C'}^{PK}$.

We note that a substantial improvement in the efficiency of this approach was achieved by [BISW17] by applying succinct non-interactive arguments (SNARG) for the verification of honest behaviour.

---

[4] Actually, the method can be simplified, as x is the input from the user , and so the user can feed it directly to the UC and homomorphically evaluate $U_x(\cdot)$ by using $FHE.Eval_{U_x,PK}(CT_{C'}^{PK})$.

4.1.2 From VBB to iO Bootstrapping

The method previously described made crucial use of the VBB property when obfuscating the conditional FHE decryption circuit, as we could think of it as a virtual black box with a perfectly hidden secret key inside. When we have access only to $\mathcal{O}_{iO}^{NC^1}$, we do not have such an explicit guarantee; this problem was overcome by [GGH+13b] by following the double-key paradigm of [NY90]. To convince ourselves that the key was indeed hidden, we would need another, functionally equivalent decryption circuit strictly without sk and then, after the iO obfuscation of both of them, the results would be indistinguishable. Intuitively, if it is infeasible to see a difference between two programs, one of which contains some information but the other does not, that means that the information did not leak, and this is what we are after.

More precisely, the structure of the bootstrapping of $\mathcal{O}_{iO}^{NC^1}$ is similar to that in the previous approach with the exception that we have to duplicate the FHE-related computations. Two public keys PK_1, PK_2 and two encryptions of C' with the different keys are provided for this, and the homomorphic function evaluation has to be executed using both of them. The conditional decryption circuit is modified to take π_1, π_2 and $CT_y^{PK_1}, CT_y^{PK_2}$ and verifies that both ciphertexts were generated honestly. If this is the case, then one of the ciphertexts is decrypted, for example by using SK_1. Note that a functionally equivalent conditional decryption circuit can now be easily constructed, which simply uses SK_2 for decryption. As $\mathcal{O}_{iO}^{NC^1}[FHE.Dec_{SK_1}^*]$ is indistinguishable from $\mathcal{O}_{iO}^{NC^1}[FHE.Dec_{SK_2}^*]$ by definition, we cannot obtain any information about the secret key.

For a formal description and further details, we refer to [GGH+13b].

4.2 Bootstrapping Obfuscation via Randomized Encodings

From a practical point of view, the existence of FHE is still a strong public-key assumption, and for most applications it is still not efficient enough. Therefore, it is natural to ask whether or not its role in bootstrapping can be relaxed . The question was first considered by Applebaum [App14a], who found a positive answer and showed that bootstrapping of VBB obfuscation can be based on a "Minicrypt"[5]-type assumption. Later, his idea was extended to the iO notion by [CLTV15, BGL+15]. We now summarize the intuitions behind these publications.

---

[5] According to Impagliazzo's terminology [Imp95], Minicrypt is an imaginary world where OWFs exist but public-key encryption is not possible.

4.2.1 The VBB Paradigm

As we have seen in §2.2.3, RE can help in compressing the private part of a complex computation and separate it from a possibly complex but publicly executable part. The high-level idea of [App14a] for bootstrapping is to obfuscate the process of preparing randomized encodings. As RE schemes are designed to make this computation as simple as possible, intuitively a limited obfuscator should suffice for this task. In hand with an obfuscated encoding algorithm for a possibly complex circuit C, on an input x, the randomized encoding $(\overline{C,x})$ can be prepared without leaking any information other than $C(x)$, according to the security of RE and the VBB obfuscator. Finally, to obtain $C(x)$ from $(\overline{C,x})$, the entirely public evaluation algorithm of the RE scheme can be used.

The only obstacle is that RE has to use fresh randomness in each encoding (i.e. for each input x) in order to guarantee security; thus randomness can be neither reused nor fixed in the obfuscated program. To evade this barrier, the necessary randomness for RE can be provided by the pseudo-random output of a PRF. For this, a modified encoding algorithm $\text{RE.Enc}^*_{\text{K},C}$ has to be obfuscated, which takes an input x, first evaluates a pseudo-random function $\text{PRF}(\text{K},x) = r$ using a hard-coded key K and then, with the help of the pseudo-random value r obtained, it computes $\text{RE.Enc}(C,x,r)$ for the hard-coded circuit C. In this way, the obfuscation of an arbitrary circuit C consist of two algorithms:

$$\mathcal{O}^{\text{P/poly}}_{\text{VBB}}[C](\cdot) = \{\mathcal{O}^{\text{TC}^0}_{\text{VBB}}[\text{RE.Enc}^*_{\text{K},C}](\cdot) = (\overline{C,\cdot}), \text{RE.Eval}((\overline{C,\cdot})) = C(\cdot)\}.$$

When the RE of [AIK06] is used, the complexity of the circuit that we need to obfuscate is dominated by the PRF, meaning that the bootstrapping works if VBB obfuscation for $\textbf{TC}^0$ can be realized.

4.2.2 The Problem of Indistinguishably Obfuscating Probabilistic Circuits

When we wish to use the approach of [App14a] to bootstrap iO, we face the problem that the encoding circuit of the RE, which we need to obfuscate, is essentially probabilistic and thus two instances of it will necessarily have different outputs on the same input. This is troublesome from the viewpoint of the definition of iO (see page 33) which explicitly considers two deterministic circuits with the same input–output behaviour. In our efforts towards a generic solution, both fixing the random coins and handling them as an extra input turn out to be dead ends. We have already seen in Applebaum's bootstrapping that random steps of a program have to remain "as random as possible"; furthermore, keeping this randomness hidden is essential for preserving security.[6]

[CLTV15] defined probabilistic iO (PiO), a generalization of iO that extends to randomized circuits as well. First, the functionality-preserving requirement (see Definition 3.1) has to be relaxed so that for any probabilistic circuit C, $\mathcal{O}_{\mathrm{PiO}}[C]$ is a deterministic circuit such that no efficient adversary can distinguish it from C based on their outputs on any input x, as long as they are run only once on each input.[7] The necessary modification of the security requirement (see Definition 3.2) is trickier: for all circuit pairs that have computationally indistinguishable output distributions on all inputs, i.e. $C_1(x) \overset{c}{\sim} C_2(x)$, it should hold that $\mathcal{O}_{\mathrm{PiO}}[C_1] \overset{c}{\sim} \mathcal{O}_{\mathrm{PiO}}[C_2]$. Based on the specific notion of indistinguishability of the distributions of probabilistic circuits, [CLTV15] defined several flavours[8] of this security requirement and also proposed a candidate construction for one of them using sub-exponentially secure iO and PPRFs.

With PiO in hand, it is straightforward to follow the basic idea of [App14a] to get the desired bootstrapping for iO:

$$\mathcal{O}_{\mathrm{iO}}^{\mathbf{P/poly}}[C](\cdot) = \{\mathcal{O}_{\mathrm{PiO}}^{\mathbf{NC}^0}[\mathrm{RE.Enc}_C](\cdot) = (\overline{C},\cdot),\ \mathrm{RE.Eval}((\overline{C},\cdot)) = C(\cdot)\}.$$

4.2.3 Full-Fledged iO from iO for Constant-Sized Circuits

The complexity measure of the bootstrapping methods used by [GGH+13b, App14a, CLTV15] was circuit *depth*, i.e. assuming logarithmic-depth ($\mathbf{NC^1}$) or even constant-depth ($\mathbf{TC}^0$) circuit obfuscation, they could accomplish the obfuscation of circuits with unbounded depth ($\mathbf{P/poly}$). Do these methods also help in reducing full-fledged obfuscation to an iO obfuscator that can only handle circuits of *limited size*?[9]

On rethinking which circuit has to be directly obfuscated in these methods, it turns out that the answer is negative. The FHE approach is promising at first sight, as the FHE decryption circuit is independent of the ciphertext length; however, its conditional version also needs to verify the steps of the evaluation function, which necessarily depends on the size of the evaluated circuit. A possible amendment was sketched in [GHRW14, §A.1] based on the ideas of [BCP14, ABG+13], which uses succinct non-interactive arguments of knowledge (SNARK) instead of non-interactive witness-indistinguishable proofs (NIWI) in order to make the verification succinct (and independent of the size of the evaluated circuit). This modifi-

---

[6] To see these points, the reader is urged to think of the task of a secure re-encryption functionality and about how could we achieve it through obfuscation.

[7] Note that the probability of computational indistinguishability is taken over the random coins of C and of $\mathcal{O}_{\mathrm{PiO}}$.

[8] The difference between the variants lies in the level of adaptivity in choosing inputs for deciding whether two circuits are indistinguishable or not, i.e. the guarantee on their obfuscations must either hold or not hold.

[9] We remark that the methods of [GIS+10] and [BISW17] achieve this property for the VBB notion.

cation also requires DiO security from the core-obfuscator, which is a rather strong assumption, especially in light of the fact that specific types of DiO and SNARK exclude each other under certain circumstances [BP15]. The size of the SNARG-based conditional FHE decryption circuit of [BISW17] is also independent of the size of the circuit to be obfuscated via bootstrapping; however, in this case, a VBB-secure core-obfuscator is required.

Regarding iO, in the RE-based solutions, the size of the encoding circuit obviously depends on the size of the circuit to be encoded, which is polynomial in its input length. At the same time, a clever implementation of this approach by [BGL$^+$15, §A] yields bootstrapping from iO for fixed-size circuits to full-fledged iO. Recall that in the bootstrapping of [CLTV15], $\mathcal{O}_{\mathrm{PiO}}^{\mathbf{NC}^1}$ is used to obfuscate a (log-depth, polynomial-size) circuit C' that prepares the randomized encoding $\overline{(C,x)}$ for any input x. The key idea is to decompose C' into a polynomial number of circuits C'_i ($i = 1, \ldots, s$) of constant size, each independent of the size of C. The use of a Program-Decomposable RE in C' (see §2.2.3) allows this, and therefore instead of obfuscating C' as a whole, each constant-sized C'_i can be obfuscated separately. If the plain RE uses r bits of randomness that are provided by a PPRF key, then now r PPRF keys will be associated with the bits of the shared randomness and each obfuscated C'_i will contain only those keys which are needed for that specific computation.

This technique allows the amplification of an iO obfuscator for constant-size circuits to full-fledged iO. From another point of view, the slowdown caused by obfuscation is also decreased from $\mathrm{poly}(|C|)$ to $|C|$ times a polynomial in the security parameter, because constant-sized circuits have to be obfuscated $s = |C|$ times.

4.3 iO from Functional Encryption: An Alternative Pathway

In this part, we deal with a type of bootstrapping that differs from the previous ones in several respects. Most notably, it does not assume an obfuscator as its starting point but instead an FE scheme (see §2.2.2); in turn, it remains enough to assume FE for functions from a weaker complexity class ($\mathbf{NC}^1$) than that of for which we aim to achieve obfuscation ($\mathbf{P/poly}$). Historically, this approach was not proposed as an amplification of existing techniques (such as those presented above), but it opened new doors towards realizing iO by showing an alternative face of the same problem. Indeed, the following results, together with the iO-based FE constructions of [GGH$^+$13b, Wat15], show the equivalence of a specific type of FE and iO up to a sub-exponential security loss (see Fig. 4.1).

As we discussed in §2.2.2, a large number of FE variants are known in the literature, some of which are implied by standard assumptions (e.g. [BJK15, GKP$^+$13, SS10]), while others necessitate the heavy hammers of either iO or GESs. Hereinafter, we are looking for answers to the following question:

what kind of FE implies iO?

As current results show, the answer depends crucially on at least two features: not surprisingly, the scope of supported functions and the efficiency of encryption. [GMM17] proved[10] that single-key FE schemes supporting function families with a short output (compared with the ciphertext length) are not capable of building iO even if non-black-box use of FE is allowed. At the same time, they also showed that non-black-box use of FE is actually indispensable for *any* transformation from FE to iO. On the positive side, it is worth noting that the transformation of [ABSV15] from FE for shallow circuits to FE for all circuits enables us to start the iO bootstrapping from FE for the complexity class $\mathbf{NC^1}$. Regarding efficiency, [BV15, AJ15] concurrently observed that single-key FE implies obfuscation if its encryption time (and ciphertext size) depends at most sub-linearly on the function size for which the secret key is issued.

We are now going to introduce three approaches [BV15, AJ15, LPST16b] (with their refinements [Lin16, LT17, KNT18a]) that lead from weakly compact FE for $\mathbf{NC^1}$ to full-fledged iO through different intermediate abstractions; these approaches are called "token-based" obfuscation, MIFE, and compact RE.

4.3.1 From FE to iO through Token-Based Obfuscation

From Token-Based iO to iO.   Token-based obfuscation [GKP+13] is a restricted form of obfuscation in which the obfuscated program can be evaluated only on encrypted tokens instead of plaintext inputs. Such a scheme consists of two algorithms. The obfuscation procedure $\text{Tok}.\mathcal{O}[C]$ outputs the obfuscation $\hat{C}$ of a circuit C and a secret key SK that is necessary for token generation, $\text{Tok}.\text{Enc}(\text{SK}, x) = \hat{x}$. Having both $\hat{C}$ and $\hat{x}$ allows the computation of $\hat{C}(\hat{x}) = C(x)$. To be non-trivial, the complexity of $\text{Tok}.\text{Enc}(.,.)$ must be independent of C and depend only on x. This restricted scheme is seemingly not useful for the the goals usual type of obfuscation, but, as [BV15] noted, it allows a so-called "input-extension" strategy that builds an obfuscator $\mathcal{O}^n$ for circuits with input length n (i.e. $x = x_1, \ldots, x_n$) from $\mathcal{O}^{n-1}$ (for ease of exposition, think of $\mathcal{O}^n$ as a VBB obfuscator):

$$\mathcal{O}^n[C](x_1, \ldots, x_n) := \{\text{Tok}.\mathcal{O}[C](x_1, \ldots, x_n),$$
$$\mathcal{O}^{n-1}[\text{Tok}.\text{Enc}_{\text{SK}, x_n=0}](x_1, \ldots, x_{n-1}),$$
$$\mathcal{O}^{n-1}[\text{Tok}.\text{Enc}_{\text{SK}, x_n=1}](x_1, \ldots, x_{n-1})\}.$$

As the complexity of Tok.Enc depends only on the (decreasing) size of its input, the above recursion can be continued such that in the last step $\mathcal{O}^1[C](x_1)$ outputs the truth table of $C(x_1)$.

---

[10] Assuming the existence of OWFs and $\mathbf{NP} \not\subseteq \mathbf{coAM}$.

From FE to Token-Based iO.   Supposing that the functional secret key FSK_C of a secret-key functional encryption (sk-FE) scheme hides circuit C, then it can be viewed as a token-based obfuscation of C, while token generation is equivalent to encryption: $Tok.Enc(SK,x) := FE.Enc(SK,x) = \hat{x}$. Consequently, the evaluation of such an obfuscated circuit is made possible by FE decryption, $FE.Dec(FSK_C, \hat{x}) = C(x)$. For Boolean circuits, [GKP+13] achieved the required function-hiding property (and so token-based obfuscation) by applying a trick similar to that of hiding the function in FHE, i.e. using UCs to first transform the function into data and then hide it with the help of the message-hiding property. In fact, the idea is more complex because Tok.Enc must produce a token $\hat{x}$, the size of which is independent of $|C|$; therefore, FE.Enc must be compact. The method of [GKP+13] to achieve this was later generalized in [BS15].

To be useful for realizing the recursive (VBB) obfuscation sketched above, the underlying FE scheme would need to be compact regardless of the output size of C (this applies for non-Boolean circuits as well). Moreover, it would need to satisfy a strong simulation-based security guarantee that was shown to be impossible by [AGVW13] as a nice analogue of VBB impossibility. [BV15] obtained token-based iO obfuscation from $(pk, 1, 1, WC)$-FE for $\mathbf{NC^1}$ circuits using similar techniques to those of [BS15] (to achieve function hiding in the public-key setting) and the PiO of [CLTV15] (which necessitates sub-exponential security of FE). The authors of [BV15] also observed that their transformation cannot be started from *any* traditional secret-key FE scheme, because their method requires the FE scheme used to remain secure even if both its encryption procedure and its key are public. To achieve this property in the secret-key setting, they proposed the notion of puncturable FE (see §2.2.2) that is sufficient for their transformation. As [KNT18a] demonstrated, $(sk^*, 1, 1, WC)$-FE is realizable without public-key primitives using (sk, m, c, NC)-FE.

4.3.2 Multi-Input FE as an Intermediate Step

From Multi-Input FE to iO.   [GGG+14] introduced the notion of multi-input FE (a.k.a. MIFE or, in our notation, $(\cdot, \cdot, m, \cdot)$-FE), which allows the function in its functional secret key to be n-ary, i.e. to take n ciphertexts as input. As they instantly observed, secret-key MIFE with a single functional key for $(n+1)$-ary functions is strong enough to imply obfuscation for circuits with input length n. The construction is rather simple:[11]

- The obfuscator first runs the set-up of the MIFE scheme, obtaining a master secret key MSK and $n+1$ encryption keys (for the different input positions).
- Using MSK, it prepares a functional secret key FSK_f for the function f, which is a UC for the circuit C that we are obfuscating (i.e. $f(x_1, \ldots, x_n, C) = C(x_1, \ldots, x_n)$).

---

[11] For more details of the construction, see [GGJS13, Theorem 18].

- Next, both the $x_i = 0$ and the $x_i = 1$ bits are encrypted for all $i = 1, \ldots, n$, resulting in $2n$ ciphertexts, $\{\mathsf{CT}_i^b\}_{i,b\in\{0,1\}}$. The last ciphertext, CT_{n+1}, is the encryption of the description of circuit C.
- The obfuscation consists of the ciphertexts and the functional key: $\mathcal{O}[C] = \{\{\mathsf{CT}_i^b\}_{i,b\in\{0,1\}}, \mathsf{CT}_{n+1}, \mathsf{FSK}_f\}$.

To evaluate $\mathcal{O}[C](x_1, \ldots, x_n)$, we only have to run the MIFE decryption on FSK_f and $\{\mathsf{CT}_i^{x_i}\}_i, \mathsf{CT}_{n+1}$, which outputs $C(x_1, \ldots, x_n)$ by its definition.

While the indistinguishability-based selective security of the underlying MIFE scheme implies iO, simulation-secure MIFE (which would imply VBB obfuscation) was proven to be impossible in [GGG+14].

From Single- to Multi-Input FE. [GGG+14] could only build the necessary MIFE scheme from iO itself, which did not help in building iO. In the secret key-setting, [BKS16] provided a transformation from any single-input FE scheme to a multi-input one (from $(sk, m, 1, NC)$-FE to (sk, m, c, NC)-FE). However, their solution is limited to a constant number c of possible inputs, because of a double-exponential security loss in c, preventing it from being applicable to the above argument. At the same time, c-input MIFE [BKS16, BLR+15, CMR17] is still sufficient for building iO for c-input circuits, and the result of [BKS16] also implies XiO, which we discuss in §4.4.2.

To reduce the necessary MIFE scheme to an assumption different from obfuscation, [AJ15] devised a so-called "arity amplification technique". With the help of a $(pk, 1, 1, WC)$-FE scheme for $\mathbf{NC^1}$, this boosts MIFE for n-ary functions to work for $(n+1)$-ary functions.

We highlight the key idea by sketching the first step of the recursive method, which builds function-hiding $(sk, 1, 2, NC)$-FE (a.k.a. 2-MIFE) from two other types of FE schemes: a $(pk, 1, 1, WC)$-FE and a function-hiding $(sk, 1, 1, NC)$-FE (e.g. from [BS15]). For clarity, we distinguish the parameters and algorithms of the two FE schemes used as building blocks as follows: bars and tildes denote the public-key and secret-key schemes, respectively. Intuitively speaking, the goal is to use the sk-FE scheme to produce a single public-key functional encryption (pk-FE) ciphertext that encrypts all the input values in a concatenated form. Such a cumulated ciphertext can then be decrypted with a functional key for a unary function that gives the same result as the original function with greater arity (which is 2 in the following simple case). The 2-MIFE scheme is (informally) determined in the following way:

- Its master key MSK consists of $\{\bar{\mathsf{PK}}, \bar{\mathsf{MSK}}, \tilde{\mathsf{MSK}}\}$, and its functional secret key FSK_f is equivalent to $\bar{\mathsf{FSK}}_{f'}$ (where f' takes a single input and $f'(x_1|x_2) = f(x_1, x_2)$).
- Encryptions for the two input positions are built differently:
  - MIFE.Enc^1 on input x_1 is actually a functional-key generation for the secret-key scheme for a function g that encrypts its input concatenated with x_1 using the public-key FE scheme (i.e. $\mathsf{CT}_1 = \tilde{\mathsf{FSK}}_g$).
  - MIFE.Enc^2 on input x_2 simply encrypts using the secret-key scheme, resulting in $\mathsf{CT}_2 = \tilde{\mathsf{CT}}$.

- MIFE.Dec is then the composition of the two decryption algorithms. First, the decryption of the secret-key scheme is executed on $CT_1 = F\tilde{S}K_g$ and $CT_2 = \tilde{C}T$, computing a ciphertext $\bar{C}T$ (encrypting $x_1|x_2$). Then this latter ciphertext is decrypted with the public-key scheme using $FSK_f = F\bar{S}K_{f'}$, giving $f(x_1|x_2)$ as we wanted.

We note that the iterative use of the public-key scheme necessitates its compactness.

4.3.3 A Classic Approach Using Compact RE

From RE to iO. Randomized encodings can be viewed as a degenerate form of obfuscation that allows evaluation only for a fixed input. This relationship between one-time and multi-time usage especially resembles the connection between PRGs and PRFs as observed by [LPST16b], who showed how to obtain obfuscation from RE. The rough idea is remarkably simple. It follows the classic method of [GGM86] for constructing a PRF from a PRG with the help of a binary tree. [LPST16b] built a tree of randomized encodings that can be defined recursively. The leaves of the tree are randomized encodings of a function (which we obfuscate) applied to all possible inputs, i.e. $F'_{x_1,\dots,x_n} = \text{RE.Enc}(F,x)$ for all $x = x_1,\dots,x_n$. In the next level, $F'_{x_1,\dots,x_{n-1}}$ are randomized encodings that generate two leaves $F'_{x_1,\dots,x_{n-1},0}$ and $F'_{x_1,\dots,x_{n-1},1}$. All the other $F'_{x_1,\dots,x_i}$ (in the upper levels) are similar randomized encodings of inputless functions that generate children, and the obfuscation of F is the root of this tree, F'. The evaluation of such an obfuscated function on input x is an iterated evaluation of randomized encodings: namely, first F' is evaluated, which gives F'_0 and F'_1, next F'_{x_1} is evaluated, and so on until $F'_{x_1,\dots,x_n}$ is reached, which evaluates to $F(x)$.

From FE to RE. This solution highlights the importance of the compactness of the RE scheme used because if the encoding time is linear in the evaluation time of $F(x)$, then obfuscation is essentially equivalent to the computation of the truth table of F. [LPST16b] showed that in the common reference string (CRS) model, for TMs, a sub-linearly compact RE scheme can be constructed from a sub-exponentially secure $(pk, 1, 1, WC)$-FE scheme for **P/poly** in a fairly straightforward way. At a high level, the encoding of a machine M and its input x is prepared with the help of the encryption algorithm for FE. The evaluation corresponds to an FE decryption with a functional secret key, issued for a proper universal circuit (the CRS is used to store this secret key). When, additionally, the sub-exponential hardness of LWE is assumed, weak compactness of the FE ciphertext suffices for the [LPST16b] transformation, while the encryption time does not need to be bounded as in other methods [BV15, AJ15]. A variant of the transformation presented by [LT17, §4.2] relaxes the security level of the assumptions but still requires their sub-exponential hardness.

Analogously to the negative result for VBB obfuscation, [LPST16b] showed that simulation-based security of compact RE is impossible to achieve in the standard model, while an indistinguishability-based notion (defined by them) is enough to get iO.

4.4 Towards the Desired Compact FE

We have seen different (non-black-box) transformations from sub-exponentially secure $(pk/sk^*, 1, 1, WC)$-FE for $\mathbf{NC^1}$ circuits to iO for $\mathbf{P/poly}$. Nonetheless, the following question remains open:

how can we achieve these notions of FE?

In this part, we discuss this question, introducing three research directions that have already provided numerous primitives, the secure realization of which would imply iO.

4.4.1 iO-Based Bootstrappable FE

In §4.1–4.2, we have seen that general log-depth circuit obfuscation implies full-fledged iO. The FE-based bootstrapping theorems previously seen raise the following question:

do we need the full power of core-obfuscators in order to realize bootstrappable FE, and through that, general-purpose iO?

iO for Constant-Degree Functions Is Enough. This question was first investigated in the pioneering work of [Lin16]. She identified a family of functions $\mathcal{F}_{\text{Lin}}$ that can be expressed as constant-degree polynomials[12] and the iO obfuscation of which implies $(pk, 1, 1, WC)$-FE if we also assume (sub-exponentially secure) LWE and $PRG \in \mathbf{NC^0}$. Additionally, the obfuscator applied needs to be "universally efficient"; this requirement can be seen as the analogue of compactness from the FE world; namely that the obfuscation time has to be independent of the degree of the computation that is obfuscated.

Her first observation is that the LWE-based $(pk, 1, 1, C)$-FE scheme of [GKP$^+$13] for Boolean functions can be bootstrapped to work for any functions with arbitrary output length, say ℓ bits, while remaining weakly compact. The idea is to issue functional secret keys for every Boolean function $f'(x, i)$ that computes the ith output bit of $f(x)$ (for all $i \leq \ell$). The critical step is that the input (x, i) has to be encrypted for all $i = 1, \ldots, \ell$, resulting in a linear dependence of the ciphertext length on the output length, which undermines the compactness of the resulting scheme. To circumvent this, the ciphertexts could be substituted by a description of the obfuscated

---

[12] The degree of $\mathcal{F}_{\text{Lin}}$ is some polynomial in the degree of the PRG used; thus it is constant if the PRG is in $\mathbf{NC^0}$.

algorithm that prepares the ciphertexts, and the size of which is independent of f. This is the encryption algorithm for Boolean FE with hard-coded x and a single input i. This concept leads us to the definition of the function family $\mathcal{F}_{\text{Lin}}$, which must be capable of computing the encryption algorithm for the Boolean FE and a PPRF that can provide the necessary randomness for encryption. While this is still not a constant-degree computation, with the help of RE, the encryption can easily be converted to be in $\mathbf{NC^0}$. The case of the PPRF is more challenging,[13] but leveraging the fact that a special-purpose PPRF for a polynomial-size domain is enough, [Lin16] designed a suitable one from a constant-degree PRG using the [GGM86] approach.

iO for Restricted-Input-Length Functions Is Useful. A different way of decreasing the generality of an obfuscator is to restrict the input length of the supported functions but not their complexity, which can still be in $\mathbf{P/poly}$. $\text{iO}^{\omega(\log\lambda)}$ and, as a special case, XiO support functions that have at most logarithmic input length in the security parameter. Supplemented with other primitives, these relaxations of obfuscation also lead to unrestricted iO (see Fig. 4.1), as shown by [BNPW16, KNT18b] in the secret-key FE setting, and using similar techniques in the public-key setting, by [LT17]. For more details, we refer to §4.4.2.

4.4.2 From Secret-Key FE to Bootstrappable FE

The second question we investigate is:

can bootstrappable FE schemes be based on ordinary (non-puncturable) secret-key FE schemes?

As it turns out, the answer is positive, and in the known transformations XiO, a surprisingly useful relaxation of iO, has a central role. First, we discuss how XiO along with other tools can help to transform secret-key FE into $(pk, 1, 1, WC)$-FE or $(sk^*, 1, 1, WC)$-FE. Finally, we touch upon the relation between secret-key FE and XiO.

From Boolean to General FE through XiO. The authors of [LPST16a] showed that XiO is powerful enough to generalize a $(pk, 1, 1, C)$-FE scheme for Boolean functions (such as that of [GKP+13], based on the LWE assumption) to work for any function. The first idea here is the same as the one described in §4.4.1 but, instead of further shaping the functions to be obfuscated, [LPST16a] applied XiO directly to the encryption algorithm of the Boolean FE and demonstrated that its efficiency suffices to obtain the desired bootstrappable $(pk, 1, 1, WC)$-FE scheme. [BNPW16] generalized this result (their method was later simplified in [KNT18b]) by showing how to build Boolean FE from plain PKE and SXiO and start the [LPST16a] transformation from this scheme instead of the FE of [GKP+13], which is tied to the LWE assumption.

---

[13] No PRF can exist in $\mathbf{NC^0}$, as it would be learnable.

Puncturable FE from Ordinary Secret-Key FE. The authors of [KNT18a] constructed $(sk^*, 1, 1, WC)$-FE in three steps. First, they took the $(pk, 1, 1, NC)$-FE of [SS10], which is based on dRE and PKE, and showed that by substituting PKE with a PPRF, $(sk^*, 1, 1, NC)$-FE can be obtained.[14]

Their second step was to transform the non-compact scheme into a collusion-succinct one. The high-level idea resembles that of [LPST16a] for turning FE for Boolean functions into a scheme that works work for any output length. To handle m functions, the single-key punctured FE scheme could be run in m instances; however, that would incur an encryption time linear in m, contradicting the requirement of collusion-succinctness. This can be avoided by, instead of preparing m ciphertexts, SXiO obfuscating the encryption circuit with a hard-wired message and giving out the result as the ciphertext.

The remaining step was to turn collusion-succinctness into weak compactness; this is achieved similarly to the method of [BV15], which we discuss in §4.4.3.

XiO from Secret-Key FE and Vice Versa. Having seen its applications, we now introduce the basic idea of [BNPW16] for building SXiO from $(sk, m, 1, NC)$-FE. Following those authors, we explain their key insight through constructing $\mathcal{O}_{\text{SXiO}'}$ for $\varepsilon = 1/2$. A naive attempt to exploit the collusion resistance of FE would be the following (still flawed) construction. Let the obfuscation consist of an FE ciphertext, encrypting the description of a circuit C (which we want to obfuscate), and for all possible inputs $x \in \{0, 1\}^n$ the functional secret keys that enable the computation of a universal circuit U_x that executes C on a hard-coded x. For evaluation, the ciphertext only has to be decrypted using the functional key that corresponds to the input. Unfortunately, in this straw-man example, the obfuscation time and size are not better than trivial, as 2^n functional keys are prepared. In order to achieve a compression factor $\varepsilon = 1/2$, the idea is to separate the input space into two parts and hard-code the first half of the input bits in the ciphertext and the other half in the functional key (for simplicity, we can assume that n is even). Since the efficiency of FE guarantees that both the encryption and the key generation time (and the size of their outputs) are bounded by $\text{poly}(|C|)$, the above obfuscation requires $2^{n/2} + 2^{n/2}$ invocations of these polynomial-time computations, achieving the desired compression. Evaluation is possible by decrypting the proper ciphertext–key pair that corresponds to the intended input, and the security of the construction follows from the selective security of the underlying FE scheme. To achieve a smaller compression factor, [BNPW16] used the (sk, m, c, NC)-FE of [BKS16], which supports functions with constant arity c (thus not implying iO directly as in [GGG+14]), allowing the separation of the input space into $c + 1$ parts (instead of the $1 + 1$ illustrated).

Assuming OWFs, [KNT18b] proved that the implication holds in the reverse direction as well, i.e. XiO implies $(sk, 1, 1, WC)$-FE, providing a way to amplify SXiO' to SXiO using OWFs through the transformation of [KNT18a] from weakly compact to collusion-resistant secret-key FE.

---

[14] Note that both dRE and PPRFs can be based on an OWF that is implied by secret-key FE.

4.4.3 Compactness, Collusion Resistance, and the Role of PRGs

Another research direction is concerned with a question about the relation between two seemingly independent properties:

> *can the collusion resistance of FE be turned into compactness?*

The answer turns out to be positive and, what is more, when we leave the firm ground of the standard assumptions and use also low-depth, super-linear-stretch PRGs (see §2.2.5) even the complexity of the required collusion-resistant FE scheme can be pushed down to the complexity of computing constant-degree polynomials.

From More Keys to Compactness.   [BV15, AJS15] showed first that the compactness of a single-key pk-FE scheme can be obtained from a non-compact pk-FE scheme that can handle multiple functional secret keys, i.e. can tolerate multiple collusions. Their idea is based on the widespread concept of using RE to represent an arbitrary computation in $\mathbf{NC^0}$. They use the opportunity to issue multiple functional keys to embed each of the decomposed functions $RE.Enc_i$ of a pdRE scheme for a circuit C into these keys. The goal is to prepare the randomized encoding $(\overline{C,x})$ by decrypting the same FE ciphertext (of the collusion-resistant scheme) which encodes input x, applying each functional secret key. Having $(\overline{C,x})$, RE.Eval can be used to derive the result of the computation (the security of which is guaranteed by the security of FE and pdRE). The crux is that $RE.Enc_i$ is essentially randomized, so, besides x, the ciphertext has to encrypt some seed s as well for a PRG that provides the necessary randomness to $RE.Enc_i$.

The functional secret key of the desired compact scheme comprises the keys of the collusion-resistant FE; its encryption algorithm is identical to the original one, while decryption works as described above. To see that the resulting scheme indeed has the compactness property, notice that while the encryption time of the starting scheme can depend on the maximum size of the functions (embedded in the keys), the pdRE scheme guarantees that the size of the *decomposed* encoding functions is independent of the size of C.

We note that the same argument can be adapted to the secret-key case. The transition from compactness to collusion resistance was shown to be possible as well by [GS16, LM16] in the public-key setting and by [KNT18a] in the secret-key setting, indicating the equivalence of these properties.

On Reducing the Complexity of the Supported Functions.   As observed by [AJS15, LV16a], the starting $(pk/sk, m, 1, NC)$-FE does not have to support general $\mathbf{NC^1}$ functions but only a PRG and the encoding function of a pdRE scheme. As pdRE is realizable in $\mathbf{NC^0}$, the existence of a polynomial-stretch PRG in $\mathbf{NC^0}$ would imply that FE for this complexity class is enough to yield iO. Polynomial stretch is required to ensure the necessary randomness for the pdRE scheme without harming the compactness of the encryption time. While this assumption leads to sufficiently simple FE schemes to start the bootstrapping, it is not implied by any standard assumptions in cryptography (see §2.2.5). At the same time, this approach clearly identifies a research direction in which some advancements may bring us closer to the secure realization of iO.

Expressing the functions as polynomials, [LV16a] showed that with the above idea, RE.Enc$_i$ (of [AIK04]) can be computed from a polynomial p_{AIK} of degree $3d_{PRG} + 2$, where d_{PRG} is the degree of the polynomial p_{PRG} describing the PRG. Recall that d_{PRG} is upper bounded by the locality L of the PRG. [Lin17, AS17] managed to further decrease the degree of the functions that the FE has to support to be bootstrappable, to L. Their key insight was that preprocessing of p_{AIK} in the encryption time is possible without harming compactness. By encrypting the tensor product $x \otimes s$ besides x and s, it is possible to do the remaining computation in degree $3L$. With clever grouping, they also managed to identify subsets of the bits of s over which by pre-computing all monomials with degree at most 3 the rest of the computation can be done in degree L, while the necessary compactness of encryption is still maintained. In view of the $L \geq 5$ lower bound [MST06], these results suggest that 5 is also a lower bound for the necessary degree that the FE needs to support. The work of [LT17] refuted this by showing further potential in the preprocessing technique. The authors of that publication bypassed the bound of 5 by noticing that the above method can also work for blocks of bits instead of single bits of the seed s. With this, they showed that by applying a $(B, \log \lambda)$-block wise local PRG, it is enough for the FE to support degree-B polynomials. As [BBKK17] observed, B might be as low as 3, but it is still an entirely open question whether such PRGs (or any objects that could substitute for them) can be based on standard assumptions.

Besides the necessary supported degree of functions, their required expressiveness can also be reduced surprisingly. In fact, a collusion-resistant FE scheme (with linear efficiency) supporting degree-d *Boolean functions* (for $d \geq 3$) is sufficient for starting the bootstrapping. The reason for this is that the decomposed elements of the encoding mechanism of pdRE produce a binary output, and exactly these elements need to be embedded in the functional secret key of the FE.

Chapter 5
Building Core-Obfuscators – In Search of a Seed I.

Having identified several primitives that imply indistinguishability obfuscation under standard assumptions (see §4, especially Fig. 4.1), we turn our attention towards the realizations of these primitives. Specifically, this section is dedicated to state-of-the-art techniques for building obfuscators for low-depth circuits (in $\mathbf{NC^1}$), which we call "core-obfuscators", denoted by $\mathcal{O}_{iO}^{\mathbf{NC^1}}$. The key question we examine in this part is:

how are current core-obfuscator candidates constructed?

We organize our discussion based on the representation of the input to the obfuscator. Accordingly, we introduce MBP obfuscators in §5.1, which historically preceded the more efficient circuit obfuscators, discussed in §5.2. The structure of our overview follows the evolution of the candidates: in §5.1.1 we start with the description of the first iO candidate of [GGH+13b], followed in §5.1.2 by the main ideas of subsequent studies that modify this construction in order to prove different flavours of security in various ideal models (see §2.3.2–2.3.4). Security in the standard model is investigated in §5.1.3.

In §5.2, we turn our attention towards efficiency considerations and introduce both core-obfuscators that mitigate the overhead caused by the MBP representation (§5.2.1) and core-obfuscators that handle circuits directly (§5.2.2). In terms of security, all of these approaches follow the same pathways as MBP obfuscators, and therefore §5.1 and §5.2 can be viewed as discussions of the security and efficiency issues, respectively (in contrast to the distinction based on the computational model). Even though our survey considers theoretical results, we summarise in a nutshell attempts of implementing these results to catch a glimpse of the distance of the current solutions from real-world applicability.

Having seen all current approaches to constructing core-obfuscators, in §5.3 we return to security issues that originate from the vulnerabilities of the GES candidates utilized (see also §2.2.4, especially Table 2.2). We discuss current attacks on core-obfuscators in §5.3.1 and also the countermeasures that have been devised in §5.3.2.

© The Author(s), under exclusive licence to Springer Nature Switzerland AG 2020
M. Horváth and L. Buttyán, *Cryptographic Obfuscation*, SpringerBriefs
in Computer Science, https://doi.org/10.1007/978-3-319-98041-6_5

Table 5.1: Comparison of core-obfuscator candidates for general circuits in $\mathbf{NC^1}$. Each candidates requires a multilinearity κ that is polynomial in the size of the obfuscated circuit. An assumption in brackets indicates that it is implied by the corresponding ideal model. The symbols $\Diamond, \Box, \bigcirc$ denote the attack categories described in §5.3.1. A cross in any of these symbols refers to the existence of an attack against all known variants of the scheme, a slash denotes that an attack threatens only the simpler variants satisfying iO security (in the case of MBP obfuscators, it means that the dual-input variant is not affected), and an empty symbol means that currently no attack is known against the candidate. Upper indices contain the specific attack type (described in §5.3.1) and lower indices denote possible countermeasures (see §5.3.2).

Candidate	Security model	Assumption	Compatible MMaps and Attacks[c]			Input	Notion
			GGH13	CLT13	GGH15		
[GGH+13b]	GCMM	(EPI)	$\otimes^5$ $\Box$ $\bigcirc$	$\otimes_1^{1,4}$ $\boxtimes_1$ $\otimes_1^4$	–	MBP	iO
[BR14b]	BR	–/BSH	$\otimes^2$ $\oslash^3$ $\oslash^3$	$\Diamond$ $\Box$ $\bigcirc$	–	MBP	iO/VBB
[BGK+14]	BGKPS	–/–	$\otimes^2$ $\oslash^3$ $\oslash^3$	$\otimes_1^{1,4}$ $\boxtimes_1$ $\oslash_1^4$	–	s/d-MBP	iO/VBB
[AGIS14]	BGKPS	–/–	$\otimes^2$ $\oslash^3$ $\oslash^3$	$\otimes_1^{1,4}$ $\boxtimes_1$ $\oslash_1^4$	–	s/d-rMBP	iO/VBB
[MSW15]	MSW-2/MSW-2/MSW-1	–/BSH'/–	$\otimes^2$ $\oslash^3$ $\oslash^3$	$\otimes_1^{1,4}$ $\boxtimes_1$ $\oslash_1^4$	–	s/d-rMBP	iO/VBB/VBB
[PST14]	Standard	SSGES	$\otimes^2$ $\oslash^3$ $\oslash^3$	$\otimes_1^{1,4}$ $\boxtimes_1$ $\otimes_1^4$	–	MBP	iO
[GLSW15]	Standard	MSE	–	$\oslash_1$ $\Box$ $\bigcirc$	–	MBP	iO
[Zim15]	BGKPS	–	–	$\boxtimes_1$ $\bigcirc$	–	Circuit	iO/VBB
[AB15]	BGKPS/BR	–	–	$\boxtimes_1$ $\bigcirc$	–	Circuit	iO
[GGH15]	–	–	–	–	$\otimes^5$ $\Box$ $\bigcirc$	MBP	iO
[BMSZ16]	BGKPS	–/–	$\otimes^1$ $\oslash^3$ $\oslash^3$	$\otimes_1^{1,4}$ $\boxtimes_1$ $\oslash_1^4$	–	s/d-gMBP	iO/VBB
[GMM+16]	MSZ/GMM+	$\exists$ PRF$\in$NC^1	$\Diamond$ $\Box$ $\bigcirc$	$\otimes_1^{1,4}$ $\boxtimes_1$ $\oslash_1^4$	–	s/d-gMBP	iO/VBB
[BD16]	BR	Sub-exp factoring	–	$\Box$ $\bigcirc$	–	Circuit	iO

For a comprehensive overview of the candidate core-obfuscators, including, for example, their compatibility with different GES types, and the applicable attacks against them, we refer to Table 5.1.

5.1 Branching Program Obfuscation

5.1.1 The Breakthrough Candidate iO Obfuscator

In this part, we reproduce an intuitive overview of the first candidate iO core-obfuscator based on the seminal work of [GGH+13b], and for further details we refer to the original publication. Without loss of generality, we restrict our attention to the obfuscation of Boolean functions with ℓ bits of input and one bit of output.[1]

The intuitive goal is to hide as much information as possible about a function and its evaluation and then argue that the resulting method fulfils Definition 3.2, of iO. As suggested earlier (see §2.1.2), we assume that the Boolean circuit C of log depth

---

[c] An up-to-date list of broken obfuscator and GES candidates is maintained at [AD].

[1] Note that every circuit C in $\mathbf{NC^1}$ can be turned into a sequence of Boolean circuits $\bar{C}(x,i) = C(x)_i$ that computes each output bit i separately and is still in $\mathbf{NC^1}$. We remark that several subsequent obfuscator candidates [AB15, Zim15, BMSZ16, Lin16] allow direct handling of circuits with multi-bit outputs.

that we would like to obfuscate has already been transformed with Barrington's method [Bar86] into an input-oblivious MBP of length n, which outputs 1 if the resulting matrix product is the identity matrix and 0 otherwise. Now our goal is to "encrypt" the sequence of matrices in the MBP in a way that still allows the evaluation of matrix products based on an evaluation function $\mathrm{inp}(\cdot)$ for all possible inputs. At the same time, the matrices should not leak any information other than the computation's output, even when observed separately or as part of any matrix products.

Randomization of the MBP. The first step towards such "encryption" is based on the randomization technique of Kilian [Kil88], originally designed to achieve secure two-party computation. The idea is to add "structured noise" to the matrices of the MBP that cancels out at the end of the computation. For this, we choose random full-rank matrices $R_i \in \mathbb{Z}_p^{5\times5}$ for $i = 1,\ldots,n-1$, compute their inverses, and envelop the matrices $A_{i,b}$ of the ith step of the MBP to form $B_{i,b} = R_{i-1}^{-1}A_{i,b}R_i$ for $b = \{0,1\}$ and all $i = 1,\ldots,n-1$, where $R_0 = R_n = I$ is the identity matrix. Intuitively, changing the matrices of the MBP to $B_{i,b}$ guarantees that the matrix product makes sense only in the right order, when the random matrices R_i cancel out. Moreover, Kilian pointed out that it is possible to statistically simulate[2] the sequence $B_{i,b}$ for all inputs x knowing only $C(x)$, which fact is a cornerstone in the security argument for most obfuscator candidates.

Unfortunately, Kilian's randomization remains secure only if those n matrices are given out that correspond to a certain input. However, we want the obfuscated program to be evaluable for any input, so it is indispensable to give out all $2n$ matrices of the MBP. [GGH+13b] observed that in this case, the possible attacks can be divided into three classes. We note that most of the MBP-based obfuscator candidates are identical up to this point but they differ in the countermeasures against these attacks.

Defence against Input Mixing. "Mixed input attacks" do not respect the evaluation function when choosing from the matrix pairs corresponding to the input bits. As Kilian's method does not force us to be consistent in our matrix choices, it is possible to select matrices corresponding to different input values even in those steps that belong to the same input bit. For instance, in the MBP in Fig. 2.1, the first and the third steps both belong to the first input bit; however, a malicious user might compute the matrix product using $A_{1,1}$ (honestly) and $A_{3,0}$ (inconsistently) even after the randomization (revealing the effect of fixing some parts of the program). To circumvent such attacks, the steps of the MBP that belong to the same input bit have to be glued together by multiplying the matrices by random scalars such that these randomnesses cancel out only when all matrices that correspond to a particular input bit are used (this is called "multiplicative bundling" in [GGH+13b]). The simplest

---

[2] For an intuition, think of $B_{1,b} = A_{1,b}R$ and $B_{2,b} = R^{-1}A_{1,b}$. With the notion $R' = A_{2,b}^{-1}R$, we find that $R = A_{2,b}R'$ and thus $B_{1,b} = A_{1,b}A_{2,b}R'$ and $B_{2,b} = R'^{-1}$, meaning that these can be generated knowing only $A_{1,b}A_{2,b}$.

way[3] to achieve this is to choose scalars $\alpha_{i,b} \in \mathbb{Z}_p$ for $A_{i,b}$ such that $\prod_{\text{inp}(i)=k} \alpha_{i,0} = 1$ and $\prod_{\text{inp}(i)=k} \alpha_{i,1} = 1$ for all fixed $k = 1, \ldots, \ell$, and compute $\alpha_{i,b} A_{i,b}$. Note that now any inconsistent matrix choice will spoil the product as the blinding scalars $\alpha_{i,b}$ will not cancel out.

Preventing Partial Evaluation.   Partial evaluation attacks can be performed to reveal whether, during evaluation with different inputs, the internal values occurring are identical. For instance, it is possible to gain information about the program by taking two different inputs and evaluating the corresponding matrix products but only until the first deviation in the matrix choices (e.g. for the MBP in Fig. 2.1, we could compare the results of the first four steps in the case of inputs $(1,0,1)$ and $(1,0,0)$). Then we can detect the equivalence of partial results in spite of Kilian's randomization, as they are the same for the matrix pairs for both of the input values 0 and 1. Note that the above bundling method is also not a sufficient countermeasure, as it might be possible to find a partial product that includes all steps that correspond to some (but not all) input bits, in which case that randomization cancels out. This vulnerability can be avoided by adding "bookends" to the beginning and end of the MBP, which make it necessary to compute the entire product because without them any partial results are incomparable. Here the idea is to add unique randomness to each matrix which can only be cancelled out by the bookends. To do this, we can increase the dimension[4] of the matrices and add the following bookends:

$$\underbrace{\left(0 * \mathbf{s}\right) \times R_0^{-1}}_{\mathbf{s}'} \times \cdots \times R_{i-1} \times \underbrace{\begin{pmatrix} * & & \\ & * & \\ & & \alpha_{i,b} A_{i,b} \end{pmatrix} \times R_i^{-1}}_{B'_{i,b}} \times \cdots \times R_n \times \underbrace{\begin{pmatrix} * \\ 0 \\ \mathbf{t} \end{pmatrix}}_{\mathbf{t}'^T},$$

where $\mathbf{s}, \mathbf{t} \in \mathbb{Z}_p^5$ and all $R_i \in \mathbb{Z}_p^{7 \times 7}$ are chosen randomly. Each $*$ denotes an arbitrary random element from $\mathbb{Z}_p$, and all the unspecified elements of the extended matrices are zero. We call $\mathbf{s}'$ and $\mathbf{t}'^T$ the bookends, and these are indeed necessary to eliminate the redundant dimensions. Kilian's matrices force us to put the bookends in place, where they allow correct evaluation if the value $\langle \mathbf{s}, \mathbf{t} \rangle$ is published in advance, as $\mathbf{s}'\left(\prod B'_{i,b}\right)\mathbf{t}'^T = \mathbf{s}\left(\prod A_{i,b}\right)\mathbf{t}^T$ is equal to $\langle \mathbf{s}, \mathbf{t} \rangle$ exactly when the matrix product is the identity.

Avoiding Algebraic Attacks.   Other attacks may try to compute non-multilinear algebraic functions over the matrices (e.g. the inverse) or not respect their algebraic

---

[3] Here we simplify the solution of [GGH+13b], where all the alphas can be chosen randomly; in our case, if q steps belong to an input bit then only $q-1$ alphas are random and one of them is determined by the constraint on their product. Otherwise the randomness can only be cancelled out by also evaluating a dummy MBP, which we wanted to avoid here for simplicity.

[4] For simplicity, we have increased the dimension only by two; however, a further increase in the dimension (by an even number) would increase the randomness in the matrices, providing an additional safeguard.

structure. To circumvent such attempts, [GGH$^+$13b] used a GES and encrypted the MBP (with the modifications described above) step by step in a way that allowed its homomorphic evaluation. For this, we can use GES candidates supporting $n+2$ tags, where zero-testing is only possible on encodings with tag T_{zt}. We encrypt the bookends and each step under different tags (denoting the encryption under tag T_k by $[\cdot]_k$),

$$[\mathbf{s}']_{T_1}, \{[B'_{i,b}]_{T_{i+1}}\}_{i\in[n],b\in\{0,1\}}, [\mathbf{s}']_{T_{n+2}}, [-\langle \mathbf{s}, \mathbf{t} \rangle]_{T_{zt}},$$

and publish them together with the corresponding evaluation function $\text{inp}(\cdot)$ as the obfuscation of the circuit C. The evaluation of $\mathcal{O}_{iO}^{\mathbf{NC}^1}[C]$ on input $\mathbf{x} = (x_1, \ldots, x_\ell) \in \{0,1\}^\ell$ uses the GES operations on the encrypted data; namely, we have to compute the following product:

$$P := [\mathbf{s}']_{T_1} \times \left(\prod_{i=1}^{n} [B'_{i,x_{\text{inp}(i)}}]_{T_{i+1}} \right) \times [\mathbf{s}']_{T_{n+2}}.$$

Note that these multiplications are valid if the tags are compatible, and then P is encoded under tag T_{zt}. The output of $\mathcal{O}_{iO}^{\mathbf{NC}^1}[C](\mathbf{x})$ is determined based on a zero-testing operation on $P + [-\langle \mathbf{s}, \mathbf{t} \rangle]_{T_{zt}}$ where both elements are encoded under the same tag so that their addition is possible, and the result is also encoded under T_{zt}; thus we can execute zero-testing. If its result is 1, then $\mathcal{O}_{iO}^{\mathbf{NC}^1}[C](\mathbf{x}) = 1$ (as the output of the MBP was the identity matrix), otherwise it is 0.

Avoiding algebraic attacks. Other attacks may try to compute non-multilinear algebraic functions over the matrices (e.g., inverse) or do not respect their algebraic structure. To circumvent such attempts, [GGH$^+$13b] uses GES and encrypts the MBP (with the above-described modifications) step by step in a way that allows its homomorphic evaluation. For this, we can use GES candidates supporting $n+2$ tags where zero-testing is only possible on encodings with tag T_{zt}. We encrypt the bookends and each step under different tags (denoting the encryption under tag T_k with $[\cdot]_k$):

$$[\mathbf{s}']_{T_1}, \{[B'_{i,b}]_{T_{i+1}}\}_{i\in[n],b\in\{0,1\}}, [\mathbf{s}']_{T_{n+2}}, [-\langle \mathbf{s}, \mathbf{t} \rangle]_{T_{zt}}$$

and publish them together with the corresponding $\text{inp}(\cdot)$ evaluation function as the obfuscation of the circuit C. The evaluation of $\mathcal{O}_{iO}^{\mathbf{NC}^1}[C]$ on input $\mathbf{x} = (x_1, \ldots, x_\ell) \in \{0,1\}^\ell$ uses the GES operations on the encrypted data, namely we have to compute the following product:

$$P := [\mathbf{s}']_{T_1} \times \left(\prod_{i=1}^{n} [B'_{i,x_{\text{inp}(i)}}]_{T_{i+1}} \right) \times [\mathbf{s}']_{T_{n+2}}$$

Note that these are valid multiplications if the tags are compatible and then P is encoded under tag T_{zt}. The output of $\mathcal{O}_{iO}^{\mathbf{NC}^1}[C](\mathbf{x})$ is determined based on a zero-test operation on $P + [-\langle \mathbf{s}, \mathbf{t} \rangle]_{T_{zt}}$ where both elements are encoded under the same tag so their addition is possible and the result is also encoded under T_{zt} thus we can execute zero-testing. If its result is 1 then $\mathcal{O}_{iO}^{NC^1}[C](\mathbf{x}) = 1$ (as the output of the MBP was the identity matrix) otherwise 0.

5.1.2 Variants Secure in Pre-zeroizing Ideal Models

Security of the obfuscator described above [GGH+13b] was argued in the fairly restrictive GCMM model, which gives an intuition of iO security rather than solid evidence. This unsatisfactory state of affairs regarding security, and the enthusiasm caused by the first positive result for obfuscation together motivated follow-up work to find more and more evidence of security. In this part, we discuss results that modify the first candidate in order to achieve security in idealized models (see §2.3.4) that assume the zero-testing to be ideal, i.e. they do not capture attacks with respect to this procedure for concrete GES candidates. For the possible interpretation of results in these models, see §2.3.3.

Towards VBB Security in the BR Model.   [BR14b] observed that the simulation-based formulation of VBB security is equivalent to iO in the case of inefficient simulation (see §3.2.2), an interpretation that is sometimes easier to work with. Taking advantage of this, the authors of [BR14b] proved iO security in the BR model by augmenting the encoding step of the [GGH+13b] obfuscator to work in the style of ElGamal encryption (following [BR13]), i.e. when encoding any matrix A under a tag T, a fresh random value r is chosen and the pair $[r]_T, [rA]_T$ is given out instead of the plain encoding $[A]_T$. This method allows the simulator to answer adversarial queries that can be interpreted as polynomials over the GES handles (see §2.3.2) of the obfuscation. These were shown to be always non-zero in the case of a non-honest query, which deviates from the rules of MBP evaluation, and thus can be easily simulated. For honest queries, the structure of ElGamal encodings lets the simulator recover the input assignment from the query, allowing the simulation in this case as well.[5] This is sufficient for iO security, but not for VBB, as the simulation might be inefficient. Indeed, if an adversary manages to query a polynomial that corresponds to some function of super-polynomially many inputs, the simulator will not be able to answer in polynomial-time.

To prevent the attacker from making such queries and to guarantee the efficiency of the simulation (leading to VBB security), the "randomizing sub-assignments" technique of [BR13] can be used. This requires $\binom{n}{3}$ additional levels in the GES, each of which is associated with a triple of variables, containing 2^3 pairs of encodings. Now, besides consistently choosing the value of every single variable, the adversary is also forced to jointly commit to the values of each triple, consistently with the single-variable choices. As shown by [BR14b], in this setting it is not possible in polynomial-time to prepare the problematic query described above without contra-

---

[5] Note that if one has access to the input, black-box access to the functionality is enough to get the correct output.

dicting BSH, proving the VBB property as long as the BSH assumption holds. We also note that an increase in the matrix dimensions from those given by [GGH$^+$13b] is not even needed to obtain the above results.

Ideal-Model VBB Security without Further Assumptions. The need for the uncertain BSH assumption was eliminated by [BGK$^+$14]. Their technique integrates previously independent defences (against input mixing, partial evaluation, and attacks that would cause inefficient simulation) into the GES encoding procedure. For this, set-based tags are used together with specially designed set systems, called "straddling sets". Such a set system is a collection of sets $\mathbb{S}_n = \{S_{i,b} : i \in [n], b \in \{0,1\}\}$ over a universe $\mathcal{U}$ such that there are only two exact covers of $\mathcal{U}$ and these are either the "zero-sets", i.e. $\bigcup_i S_{i,0}$, or the "one-sets", i.e. $\bigcup_i S_{i,1}$.

Example 5.1 ([BGK$^+$14]^6). Over the universe $\mathcal{U} = \{1,2,3,4,5\}$, let the straddling set system $\mathbb{S}_3$ be the following:

$$S_{1,0} = \{1\}, S_{2,0} = \{2,3\}, S_{3,0} = \{4,5\},$$

$$S_{1,1} = \{1,2\}, S_{2,1} = \{3,4\}, S_{3,1} = \{5\}.$$

Consequently, if all matrices of an MBP that correspond to the same input bit position are encoded under the zero- and one-sets of the same straddling set system, then input mixing would involve elements that were encoded under non-disjoint sets, thus prohibiting multiplication in the GES. This supersedes the use of $\alpha_{i,b}$ for randomizing the matrices (cf. §5.1.1), but does not substitute the randomness needed for the ElGamal-like usage of a GES.

To also evade partial evaluation and attacks causing inefficient simulation, the above idea can be enhanced by using d-MBPs. In these, the matrices represent two input positions,[7] and this is handled by merging the corresponding sets of different straddling set systems. Encoding the matrices under the resulting interlocking sets forces the adversary to always commit to a specific input, thus substituting for the role of the "randomizing sub-assignments" technique and the BSH assumption in the proof of VBB security.

Other Candidates. [MSW15] investigated the capabilities of obfuscation in less restrictive models than BR or BGKPS in terms of the allowed operations. They proposed two models and extended unconditional generic VBB security to the MSW-1 model, unconditional *iO* security to the MSW-2, model and VBB security to the MSW-2 model, assuming that the BSH$'$ holds. Interestingly, they also observed that any unconditional proof of the latter claim would entail proving the algebraic analogue of P$\neq$NP. Their key tool is a strengthening of straddling set systems, in which each zero-set has non-empty intersection with all one-sets.

---

[6] For the general version of this example, see [BGK$^+$14, Appendix A].

[7] Without loss of generality, it can be assumed that the evaluation functions of the MBP fulfil some requirements; for example, none of the input bit positions is ignored and it is not equivalent to a single-input MBP.

We mention one more candidate core-obfuscator, proposed by [GGH15], that adapts the original [GGH$^+$13b] candidate to the GGH15 graph-induced GES, although without a formal proof of security.

5.1.3 Core-Obfuscators in the Standard Model

As already discussed in §2.3, the ultimate goal regarding security is to prove that obfuscation is secure in the standard model under standard assumptions. This part is dedicated to core-obfuscator candidates that are approaching this goal.

The security (or an intuition of it) of the [GGH$^+$13b] obfuscator follows directly from the EPI assumption (in the standard model); that is, however, explicitly tied to the construction, making it less persuasive (see §2.3.1). We introduce three other arguments in the standard model, which rely on the SSGES, SSGES', or MSE assumption. These seemed to be plausible when they were introduced, but later attacks (discussed in §5.3) revealed that none of them is supported by current GES candidates.

iO from Semantically Secure GESs.   [PST14] first reduced the security of iO to a succinct and general assumption about the underlying GES, namely the SSGES assumption. They introduced an intermediate abstraction, called neighbouring-matrix iO (NMiO), that requires the indistinguishability of only those obfuscated MBPs that are not just functionally equivalent but differ only in a constant number of matrices. This new notion was then shown to be realizable by a simplified variant of the [BGK$^+$14] obfuscator based on semantically secure graded encodings. As discussed in §2.3.1, the SSGES assumption considers certain "valid" message distributions, and [PST14] justified the validity of the distributions used with the help of a generic security analysis. The desired iO notion is achieved through a construction-independent transformation from NMiO to iO without further assumptions. The key tool of the transformation is a merging procedure that takes two MBPs P_0, P_1 and a bit b, the value of which affects only a constant number of matrices in the output $\text{Merge}(P_0, P_1, b)$ that evaluates P_b. Let $\mathcal{O}_{iO}[P] = \mathcal{O}_{\text{NMiO}}[\text{Merge}(P, D, 0)]$, where D denotes a dummy MBP computing the constant function 1. The indistinguishability of $\mathcal{O}_{iO}[P_0]$ and $\mathcal{O}_{iO}[P_1]$ for functionally equivalent P_0 and P_1 is proved through a hybrid argument based on the properties of NMiO and the merging procedure.[8]

In order to reduce the security to the more favourable SSGES' assumption, [PST14] adapted the above technique to the merge procedure of [BCP14] for circuits and to another abstraction called "neighbouring-input" iO, which relaxes iO in the same style as NMiO.

---

[8] In the hybrid steps, the MBPs are replaced matrix by matrix in the following manner: $\text{Merge}(P_0, D, 0) \dashrightarrow \text{Merge}(P_0, P_1, 0) \rightarrow \text{Merge}(P_0, P_1, 1) \dashrightarrow \text{Merge}(P_1, P_1, 1) \rightarrow \text{Merge}(P_1, P_1, 0) \dashrightarrow \text{Merge}(P_1, D, 0)$. Note that after each merged MBP has been NMiO obfuscated, all the subsequent hybrid steps become indistinguishable, while the first and the last steps correspond to the iO of P_0 and P_1.

Building on the Subgroup Elimination Assumption. [GLSW15] proposed a different approach to building iO in the standard model, using composite-order GESs and a fairly natural assumption about them. Their idea is to run parallel obfuscations concurrently, which is enabled by the CRT for a composite-order GES, opening the door to separate handling of different inputs by different obfuscator instances in the security proof. The goal of such input isolation is to be able to invoke Kilian's information-theoretic argument [Kil88] about randomized MBPs. Recall that in ideal-model proofs Kilian's theorem is used to simulate the obfuscated MBP from the point of view of the input (which implies the output through oracle access to the functionality). In contrast, now it is used to switch – invisibly to the adversary – the underlying MBP to another functionally equivalent one for one specific input. Doing this for all inputs through a sequence of 2^n hybrids (where n is the input length) allows us to argue iO security (i.e. that the obfuscations of functionally equivalent MBPs are indistinguishable) of the obfuscator. The key challenge in this is the actual isolation of inputs. Considering one input, the goal is to evaluate that specific input using a specific obfuscated instance and eliminate all the other parallel instances by zeroing them out. To do this securely (for all inputs), [GLSW15] built on the MSE assumption, which intuitively claims that under certain circumstances it is hard to distinguish a zero element from a random element in a particular subgroup.

We remark that, according to an informal argument of [GLSW15], in order to prove iO security, the sub-exponential hardness of any instance-independent assumptions seems inevitable (as in the case of $SSGES'$ and MSE).

5.2 Improving Efficiency: From MBP to Circuit Obfuscation

Up to this point, all the obfuscator candidates that we have introduced convert their input into an MBP first, as the actual steps of the obfuscation were designed for this model of computation. The transformation of Barrington [Bar86] confirms that this is indeed possible; however, its price is an exponential growth of the MBP length (at most by 4^d) in the circuit depth d. While this remains polynomial if the circuit is from $\mathbf{NC^1}$, the efficiency loss is obvious even in this case. When we start to care also about realizability besides the existence of general-purpose obfuscators, this unsatisfactory state of affairs raises the natural question of *whether it is possible to minimize the size of the MBP before obfuscating it.* The answer is crucial, especially as the MBP length determines the necessary multilinearity κ of the GES used. It is favourable to keep κ low because the encoding size depends polynomially on it and also because – intuitively – a smaller κ could be easier to realize under standard assumptions.

More radically, we could even ask:

is it essential to obfuscate MBPs, or are circuits also obfuscatable directly?

In this part, we investigate the sources of inefficiencies in previous constructions and introduce the current approaches towards practically usable methods. We show that the answers are positive for both of the above questions. Finally, we review the available implementations; this properly illustrates the distance of the theoretical results from concrete applicability.

5.2.1 Improving Efficiency by Minimizing MBP Size

A straightforward first attempt to reduce the MBP length might be to "balance" the depth d of the formula or circuit before Barrington's transformation. The best we can achieve in this direction is depth $d = 1.82 \log s$, following [PM76], where s is the length of the formula, although after the transformation this still leads to a length-$s^{3.64}$ MBP. As it turns out, for further optimization, we have to bypass two key tools of the previous solutions.

Avoiding Barrington's Theorem.   [AGIS14] proposed the first solution without needing to invoke Barrington's theorem. Starting from a Boolean formula (that is, a fan-out-1 Boolean circuit), they showed a transformation to a so-called relaxed MBP (rMBP), defined by them. In an rMBP, permutation matrices are replaced by general *full-rank* matrices over a finite field and the output of the computation is determined by the value of a fixed entry in the matrix product. The advantage of the relaxed notion is twofold. It allows a more efficient conversion from formulas than the one given by Barrington, and it is still sufficient to adapt the [BGK+14] obfuscator construction and security argument. The key insight of the transformation is that the evaluation of a Boolean formula can be turned into a graph connectivity problem in a certain directed graph, which in turn can be interpreted as matrix multiplication. This solution reduces the length of the rMBP to $O(s)$; however, the dimension of the matrices increases to $O(s)$.

Bypassing Kilian's Theorem.   The reason why the matrix dimension is high can be traced back to the use of the randomization theorem of Kilian [Kil88], which requires the matrices of the MBP to have full rank and thus to be invertible. [BMSZ16] interpreted the necessity of invertibility as meaning that information about the actual state (represented by a matrix) cannot be forgotten, and asked the question of *whether it is possible to directly obfuscate programs that can "forget"* (i.e. the matrices in their MBP representation are not full rank). By eliminating the use of Kilian's theorem with an equivalent randomization, they adapted the [AGIS14] obfuscator to also work for more general MBPs than before (denoted by gMBP). Namely, the matrices are allowed to be non-invertible, and even rectangular (with compatible dimensions) with the only restriction being that no partial product of them should result in an all-zero matrix (i.e. they must be "non-shortcutting" in the terminology of [BMSZ16]). This leads to a faster evaluation time (due to the decreased matrix dimensions) and, for the first time, enables the obfuscated program to output *multi-*

ple bits simultaneously (in different entries of the product matrix), eliminating the need for running different MBPs to compute each output bit.

5.2.2 Direct Obfuscation of Circuits

Instead of improving MBPs before the actual obfuscation, in concurrent and independent publications, [AB15] and [Zim15] proposed a radically new approach: to obfuscate arithmetic circuits directly. Their basic idea is to take a universal circuit $U(C,x)$ and, with the help of a GES, encode every bit of C and both 0 and 1 values for each input bit of x. An evaluator can then homomorphically evaluate $U(C,x)$ by using the appropriate encodings for each input bit and zero-test the resulting encoding(s) to obtain the output (which may consist of multiple bits). Input consistency can be enforced by using straddling sets as before, so the source of difficulty is the freedom of the evaluator in terms of the evaluated function. Namely, one still can deviate from computing U, but that is circumvented by the use of a composite-order GES (see §2.2.4). This allows us to encode vectors instead of scalar values. For each encoded vector, set its dimension to two such that the first vector element always corresponds to a value used in the computation (the bits of C and x) while the second vector element is always some random value r_i. These are bound together by the nature of composite-order GESs. Evaluating U on such encodings results in an encoding vector $(U(C,x),R)$, where $R = U(r_1,\ldots,r_{|C|+|x|})$ is a random value. To make the result of the honest computation of C (but nothing else) derandomizable, the encoding of $(1,R)$ can be given out and compared with the result using a zero-test.

Unfortunately, straightforward homomorphic evaluation is still not possible, as additions in GESs are possible only between encodings with the same tag, but the bits of C and x are necessarily encoded with different tags. In order to get around this, ElGamal encodings of each bit can be used instead of plain encodings, as was done in [BR14b] (see §5.1.2). The addition of these encodings is doable by performing three multiplications and an addition of encodings under the same tag.[9]

While these basic ideas are common to [AB15, Zim15] and also occure in the circuit obfuscator candidate of [BD16], each of these publications proposed a refined variant as well. [Zim15] achieved VBB security in the BGKPS model. In contrarast, [AB15] proved only iO security, but in the more challenging BR model, at the cost of needing input length n plus two slots in the GES encodings. This efficiency loss was reduced by [BD16], requiring only three slots, assuming the sub-exponential hardness of factoring.[10] We note that [Lin16, DGG+16] also built obfuscators start-

---

[9] Let $X_i = [r_i]_{T_i}, Y_i = [r_i m_i]_{T_i}$ be the ElGamal encoding of m_i with tag T_i, where r_i is random. Then the encoding of $m_1 + m_2$ can be computed as $X_1 X_2 = [r_1 r_2]_{T_1 + T_2}, X_1 Y_2 + X_2 Y_1 = [r_1 r_2(m_1 + m_2)]_{T_1 + T_2}$.

[10] The additional assumption is due to the fact that the order of the composite-order ring is not hidden as in the other cases.

ing from these ideas; however, these were designed for a more restricted circuit class (see the discussion in §6.2).

Skipping the transformation to an MBP before the actual obfuscation leads to significant improvement in terms of the obfuscation size and evaluation time, which are – for the first time – not exponential but only quadratic in the circuit depth d (for keyed functions,[11] in which hiding the key suffices, performance can be further improved). In light of these facts, one could ask whether we still need bootstrapping or whether we could directly obfuscate any circuit in $\mathbf{P/poly}$. Unfortunately, the noise growth of current approximate MMaps prevents us from being able to directly obfuscate circuits outside of $\mathbf{NC^1}$; thus, as [Zim15] pointed out, "finding *clean* (and secure) MMaps is not only a technicality but one of the most fundamental open problems in cryptography".

5.2.3 Implementing Obfuscation

We close our review of efficiency considerations by illustrating the performance of known obfuscation solutions through current implementation results. As our goal is merely to illustrate the distance of the (obviously theoretical) results from applicability, we are not going into optimization details, but will only sketch the milestones achieved in improving performance and the functions obfuscated.

The first executable[12] implementation of obfuscation was due to [AHKM14]. A 16-bit point function (containing 15 AND gates) was the most complex function that they were able to obfuscate after the implementation of ideas from [AGIS14, BGK+14, BR14a]. The process took 9 hours and resulted in an obfuscated program of size 31.1 GB, the evaluation of which on a single input took around 3.3 hours on a machine with 32 cores and 244 GB RAM.[13]

[LMA+16] proposed a unified framework, called 5Gen[14] [5GE], for implementing GESs and realized the obfuscator of [BMSZ16], roughly halving the costs seen above. For the first time, a circuit obfuscator [Zim15] was realized as well but, for the point-function application investigated – which was not representative – it was not competitive with the other approach.[15] First, [CMR17] managed to run circuit obfuscators on more complex inputs; namely, they obfuscated a PRF with a 64-bit

---

[11] Obfuscating keyed functions is actually enough for bootstrapping and thus for obfuscating all circuits.

[12] In the implementation of [BOKP15], the estimated obfuscation time of a 2-bit multiplication circuit is about 10^{27} years and it would require 20 zettabytes of memory.

[13] [BHLN15] showed several techniques to speed up the evaluation and, in fact, they managed to break the "point obfuscation challenge" (announced at the CRYPTO-2014 rump session [AHKM14]) in just 19 minutes using a cluster of 21 PCs.

[14] Referring to MMaps as the fifth generation of cryptography after symmetric-key encryption, PKE, bilinear maps, and FHE.

[15] This is due to the fact that the necessary multilinearity is at least double the input length in the case of [Zim15]; this cost is exaggerated by the simplicity of point functions.

key and a 16-bit input with the same order of magnitude of obfuscation time, size, and evaluation time (but for a more complex function). [HHSS17] implemented the first obfuscator based on a GGH15-based GES (with certain simplifications) and ran it on a finite state machine with 100 states with a 68-bit input length.

5.3 The Impact of GES Vulnerabilities on Core-Obfuscators

Candidate multilinear maps and the assumptions about them have been threatened by various attacks since the beginning owing to the lack of a security reduction to a well-established cryptographic assumption. Initially, the so-called zeroizing attacks affected only those applications that required a public encoding mechanism (like that in multi-party key exchange), but these were extended later to work also in the secret-key setting that is utilized in the obfuscator candidates. However, these attacks all involve multiple encodings of zero at the zero-testing (top) level that must be obtained by multiplying lower-level encodings with a certain structure. Since obfuscation of programs allows zeros to be produced only in a restricted way (as a result of "honest evaluation"), it is highly non-trivial to apply these attacks to iO candidates. Nevertheless, several publications have demonstrated that this is indeed possible if the zero-testing operation is not idealized to return a binary value, representing the invalidity of several assumptions (see Table 2.3) and of the "pre-zeroizing models" (see Table 2.4).

5.3.1 Current Attacking Strategies

As we are considering general-purpose iO, finding even a single pair of equivalent circuits (or MBPs) that are distinguishable after obfuscation is enough to break iO security. To characterize attacks,[16] we can sort them into three categories depending on the generality of the programs the obfuscation of which is vulnerable. These can be specific MBP classes that are obfuscated directly (denoted by $\diamond$ in Table 5.1), general circuits from $\mathbf{NC^1}$ that are obfuscated either directly or using an MBP obfuscator after applying Barrington's transformation or the transformation that is part of the candidate ($\square$), or, finally, general polynomial-size circuits ($\bigcirc$). Practically, the latter means that the obfuscation of any of the bootstrappable functions (see Table 4.1) must be vulnerable. In a bird's-eye view, the following attacks are known at the time of writing (see also Table 5.1):

1. [CGH+15] presented the first attack affecting the CLT13-based MBP obfuscator candidate of [GGH+13b] and the simple variants of [AB15, Zim15]. Regarding MBP obfuscation, this attack requires the obfuscation of MBPs computing the

---

[16] In this, we follow [AJN+16, Appendix A], which provided the first (now outdated) summary of attacks.

constant-one function,[17] where the input bits are partitioned into three sets such that the MBP is also decomposable into three steps, each depending only on the corresponding input partition. This special structure is not guaranteed if an MBP is obtained from the Barrington transformation; consequently, this attack can be avoided if the obfuscator takes a circuit and uses the transformation as part of the process. Circuit obfuscators are broken for functions as simple as point functions.

2. The so-called "Annihilation attacks" of [MSZ16] thwart both the single- and the dual-input variants of the GGH13-based obfuscators of [BR14b, BGK+14, AGIS14, MSW15, PST14, BMSZ16]. The high-level idea is to take two MBP descriptions of the constant zero-functionality and evaluate their obfuscation several times to obtain multiple results of successful zero-tests. In fact, these results are ring elements (and not binary values as assumed by several idealized models) which contain information about the evaluated MBP. This information allows us to distinguish the obfuscations after finding an annihilating polynomial of the zero-test results of one MBP that does not annihilate the zero-test results of the other.

3. [ADGM17] generalized Attack 2 to make it work also for circuits, as opposed to simple MBPs. To do so, they identified a property of two single-input MBPs, called "partial inequivalence", that is sufficient for the generalized attack. The authors of [ADGM17] also demonstrated that transforming certain circuits via Barrington's method yields partially inequivalent MBPs and, in particular, these include certain UCs enabling the attack of obfuscations of bootstrappable functions (see Table 4.1) as well. The attack, however, does not extend to the dual-input MBP technique.

4. Observing a matrix identity, [CLLT17] managed to extend Attack 1 to work for MBPs with any structure. Importantly (and contrary to Attack 2), their approach does not rely on the algebraic structure of the encoded matrices, and thus extends to all single-input MBP obfuscators based on the CLT13 GES, including those of [GGH+13b] and [GMM+16], showing the vulnerability of the MSZ model.

5. [CGH17] extended Attack 2 to work also for the [GGH+13b] obfuscator over either the GGH13 or the GGH15 GES. This is achieved by obtaining information about the "multiplicative-bundling" scalars (see §5.1.1) through the zeroizing techniques of [CHL+15, CLLT16] (relying on input partitioning) and then using the extension of Attack 2 in the GGH13 setting. In the case of GGH15, the scalars can be recovered in sub-exponential time (or quantum polynomial-time), allowing an input-mixing attack.

5.3.2 Countermeasures

While some of the above attacks can be easily circumvented (e.g. by not obfuscating MBPs directly but obfuscating circuits instead, via Barrington's transformation),

---

[17] Note that this leads to a successful zero-test as the last step of the evaluation of the obfuscated program (see §5.1.1).

real countermeasures are essential not only to evade the attacks, but also to understand their nature and to design more robust constructions towards the ultimate goal of reducing iO security to standard assumptions (see the discussion in §2.3.1).

As a first step, [CGH+15, MSZ16, GMM+16] devised idealized models (see the MSZ and GMM+ models in §2.3.4) that give a more accurate abstraction of the zero-testing procedure of current GES candidates, capturing most of the above attacks (for an exception, see Attack 4). [GMM+16] proposed the first scheme that was proven secure in such a weaker idealized model under the assumption that a PRF exists in $\mathbf{NC^1}$. Their construction builds on the techniques of the [BGK+14] obfuscator with a crucial modification before the first step. Namely, the obfuscated MBP is extended to consist of block-diagonal matrices, where in one block the original MBP is computed while in the other one a PRF on the same input is computed. This "self-fortification" technique allows us to argue that no annihilating polynomial can be computed over zero-test results, because otherwise it could be used to efficiently distinguish between the PRF and a truly random function. In the context of circuit obfuscators, [DGG+16] implemented the same defence strategy (see §6.2).

We also mention a generic countermeasure that turns an input program to the obfuscator, possibly with properties that make its obfuscation vulnerable, into another one without those sensitive properties. Unfortunately, such a solution, to the best of our knowledge, is only known against input partitioning, but it would be desirable to avoid other vulnerabilities as well (e.g. partial inequivalence). This countermeasure is as follows.

1. [FRS17] proposed a technique called "input stamping" to immunize the obfuscator against input-partitioning attacks (Attacks 1 and 4) on [CLT13]-based obfuscators. The key idea is to extend the input space of a program P to be obfuscated by substituting it with a program Q that returns 0 on an input z if and only if z has the form $x|S(x)$, where S is a "stamping function" satisfying certain properties (that thwart input partitioning), and $P(x) = 0$, from which the original output is recoverable if the stamp is correct.

Finally, we mention that in order to gain confidence in standard-model security proofs it would be essential to come up either with new assumptions that are plausible using current GES candidates or with more robust GESs.

Chapter 6
Building Functional Encryption: In Search of a Seed, II

In this section, we continue introducing candidate realizations of bootstrappable primitives, now focusing on those ones that yield full-fledged iO through constructing an FE scheme first. The main benefit of this approach is that – up to now – it has led to a better characterization of the problem of building iO. By eliminating the better-understood parts, it is enough to start bootstrapping from simpler primitives than the core-obfuscators seen in §5. The pioneering work of [Lin16] showed that bootstrappable FE can be built using MMaps with constant multilinearity (κ), whereas all previous core-obfuscators required κ to be polynomial in the size of the obfuscated circuit. This and follow-up work brought the necessary MMaps closer to reality than ever and also identified the price of the improvement: *when we decrease the multilinearity to get closer to the standard assumption $\kappa = 2$, we have to rely more and more on the non-standard assumption that super-linear-stretch PRGs exists with constant locality* (we have seen the latter in §4.4.1 and §4.4.3). At the time of writing, this line of research has managed best to characterize the problem of basing iO on standard assumptions. According to this, finding 3-linear maps and a $(3, \log \lambda)$-blockwise local PRG with super-linear stretch based on standard assumptions would lead to iO based on standard assumptions [LT17].

While we are interested in the same security and efficiency aspects of the constructions introduced as in the previous section, the following discussion is structured quite differently. The reason is that the subsequent solutions are less coherent than the various core-obfuscators, and thus we organize our introduction based on the realized primitives, from which bootstrapping can be started. These include different FE variants and also iO obfuscators, which deviate from core-obfuscators in the generality of circuits they are able to handle. In fact, we now consider a remarkably conscious approach to the design of special-purpose iO to secure only that specific functionality which is required for bootstrapping (in contrast to the limited but still general class $\mathbf{NC^1}$).

Another important difference compared with core-obfuscators is that ideal-model solutions turn out to be less interesting. The reason is that the transformations from weakly compact FE schemes to iO (i.e. the essential step we always have to go through; see Fig. 4.1) require the non-black-box use of FE (see §4.3), and thus mod-

M. Horváth and L. Buttyán, *Cryptographic Obfuscation*, SpringerBriefs in Computer Science, https://doi.org/10.1007/978-3-319-98041-6_6

elling any building blocks with oracles is insufficient for bootstrapping purposes. Indeed, [GMM17] proved that some sort of non-black-box technique is inherent in any transformation from FE to iO.

Last but not least, no direct attacks are known against most of the following constructions (an exception is the FE scheme of [GGHZ16]); however, almost all of the assumptions used are known to be false (see Table 2.3), a state of affairs that is rather worrisome. Nevertheless, these false assumptions (at the time of writing) clearly identify research directions in the field of MMap and GES design.

We discuss the following bootstrappable primitives: collusion-resistant pk-FE in §6.1 (the design of which historically preceded the bootstrapping techniques using FE), special-purpose obfuscators in §6.2, secret- and public-key FE for low-degree polynomials in §6.3, and, finally, PAFE in §6.4. For a concise summary of these solutions, we refer to Table 6.1.

Table 6.1: Comparison of candidate schemes that can be used for FE-based bootstrapping. κ denotes the required multilinearity, and d is the maximum degree of supported polynomials for the scheme achieved. A security model in brackets indicates that security has been proven in the standard model under the corresponding assumption that is implied by the given model, showing some evidence of its validity.

Candidate	Security model	Assumption	Compatible MMaps	κ	Function class	Achieved notion
[GGHZ16]	Standard	GGHZ	CLT13	poly($|C|$)	$\mathbf{NC^1}$	$(pk,m,1,NC)$-FE
[Lin16]	BR/standard	$-$/SSGES	CLT13	$O(1)$	$\mathcal{F}_{\mathrm{Lin}}$	iO
[DGG$^+$16]	MSZ	$-$	GGH13	$O(1)$	$\mathcal{F}_{\mathrm{Lin}}$	iO
[CMR17]	BGKPS	$-$	CLT13	$O(1)$	$\mathcal{F}_{\mathrm{Lin}}$	iO
[LV16a]	Standard	jSXDH	GGH13/CLT13/	$2d$	Deg-d, Boolean	$(sk,m,1,L)$-FE
[LV16a]	Standard	jSXDH	GGH15	$2d$	Deg-d, Boolean	$(pk,m,1,L)$-FE
[Lin17]	Standard	SXDH	MMaps	d	Deg-d, Boolean	$(sk,m,1,L)$-FE
[AS17]	(BGKPS)	AS	GGH13/CLT13	d	Deg-d, Boolean	PAFE

6.1 Collusion-Resistant FE from the GGHZ Assumption

Constructions of FE for general functions had only been known based on iO [GGH$^+$13b, Wat15] when [GGHZ16] proposed a $(pk,m,1,NC)$-FE candidate based on a composite-order GES. This result, complemented by the bootstrapping theorems of [BV15, AJS15], established the equivalence of the two primitives up to a sub-exponential security loss.

To build collusion-resistant FE, [GGHZ16] utilized techniques that were originally designed to realize core-obfuscators. Their high-level strategy is to take a UC for $\mathbf{NC^1}$ and transform it first to an MBP, which is randomized with similar techniques to those used in obfuscation. The public key of their FE scheme consists of those matrix pairs that correspond to the input bit positions (i.e. do not belong to a program description). Encryption is done by choosing the matrices according to the bits of the plaintext, and re-randomizing and "bundling" them. Functional secret keys are generated analogously, but using the matrices of the program description. A message and a key together with the UC form a program that can be evaluated during decryption. One of the challenges implied by this approach is that the re-randomization and bundling need to be a public procedure (unlike in obfuscation), but the resulting ciphertexts should still be such that it is not possible to mix their parts. This was not enabled by previous techniques (which allow either anyone to create encodings under any tag or no one to do so without the master key), so a new procedure was proposed to extend the functionality of GESs (especially that of [CLT15]) to achieve the required functionality.

This high-level idea was implemented by realizing an intermediate abstraction called slotted FE, where "slots" are achieved using a composite-order GES and serve similar purposes to those in some core-obfuscators.

The security of the final scheme is based on the GGHZ assumption and the security of PPRFs in $\mathbf{NC}^1$. Unfortunately, the former assumption was explicitly broken by [CGH+15] with an attack based on the same idea as Attack 1 described in §5.3.1.

6.2 iO from Constant-Degree GESs

In terms of realizability, the GES is the Achilles heel of all obfuscator constructions, and none of the approaches we have introduced so far has managed to decrease significantly the role of this building block. [Lin16] took the first step towards this important goal by identifying a function family $\mathcal{F}_{\mathrm{Lin}} \in \mathbf{NC}^0$, the iO obfuscation of which both is bootstrappable (see §4.4.1) and can be realized using only constant multilinearity as opposed to a polynomial in the obfuscated function's size.

6.2.1 Circuit Obfuscation with a Constant Number of Multiplications

While for $\mathbf{NC}^0$ circuits iO is trivial,[1] to be useful for bootstrapping (see §4.4.1) it has to fulfil a stricter efficiency requirement, namely, the obfuscation time has to be universal, i.e. independent of the actual degree of the computation. The starting point of the universally efficient $\mathcal{O}_{\mathrm{iO}}^{\mathcal{F}_{\mathrm{Lin}}}$ of [Lin16] is the (arithmetic) circuit obfuscator of [AB15] (§5.2.2). Recall that [AB15] needed a much higher degree of mul-

---

[1] One could output the truth table of a function as the obfuscation.

tilinearity[2] than the degree of the obfuscated U owing to the use of straddling sets and the method of handling additions. In order to mitigate this overhead, [Lin16] argued that when the domain of the obfuscated circuit is a set of properly chosen "symbols", the bits of each input symbol can be encoded under the same tag using the same ElGamal randomness. As a result, the addition of these encoded bits – which are said to have the same *type* – is possible without turning addition into multiplication.[3] The question arises, *for which circuits does this trick save enough multilinearity?* Towards the characterization of the necessary properties of such circuits, [Lin16] defined the so-called "type-degree" of a circuit recursively: the type of the outgoing wire of a gate is equal to that of the incoming wires if those are identical, otherwise[4] the type of the incoming wires add up. The analysis of Lin shows that κ is proportional to the type-degree of the obfuscated circuit, which is the sum of the output wire types. As the type-degree of $\mathcal{F}_{\text{Lin}}$ is constant, it can be obfuscated with the modified [AB15] method using a constant κ. While the original scheme of [AB15] is secure in an ideal model, [Lin16] also argued security of her special-purpose obfuscator in the standard model under a variant of the SSGES' assumption of [PST14].

6.2.2 Further Refinements

We note that [CMR17] (see their construction called "Linnerman") managed to further decrease the constant κ by adapting the ideas of [Lin16] to the circuit obfuscator of [Zim15].

A common weakness of these solutions is that they both involve an exponential noise growth in the CLT13 GES used, owing to the structure (related to straddling sets) of the encodings contained in the obfuscation. To obtain polynomial noise growth, besides constant multilinearity in $\mathcal{O}_{\text{iO}}^{\mathcal{F}_{\text{Lin}}}$, [DGG+16] devised a way to use a composite-order variant of the GGH13 GES in a specific manner (they proposed two techniques that were later shown to be vulnerable by [DPM17], in which work, however, another countermeasure was proposed). Besides noise reduction, stronger ideal-model security was also achieved in [DGG+16] with the help of the self-fortification strategy of [GMM+16]. The original idea was implemented in the circuit obfuscator using some slots of the composite-order GES to evaluate a PRF on the input. The result of this additional computation randomizes the zero-test output sufficiently but can be cancelled out without affecting the result of the intended computation.

---

[2] More precisely, $n \cdot 2^{\text{depth}(U)}$, where n is the input size of U, that is, $|C| + |x|$. This growth is the reason why the [AB15] obfuscator was limited to **NC^1** circuits.

[3] The sum of $(R = [r]_T, X_1 = [rm_1]_T)$ and $(R = [r]_T, X_2 = [rm_2]_T)$ is $(R = [r]_T, X_1 + X_2 = [r(m_1 + m_2)]_T)$.

[4] When multiplication is needed, that increases the degree.

6.3 FE for Low-Degree Polynomials from SXDH

Some kind of abstraction of obfuscation has always appeared in the constructions of bootstrappable primitives seen above (the FE scheme of [GGHZ16] is an exception, but this construction also builds on techniques similar to core-obfuscators). [LV16a] pointed out that this is not inherent and that simpler concepts are enough to build the desired objects. However, this result and follow-up work have not managed to also eliminate the use of GESs, although in some sense they have successfully reduced their role in the constructions.

6.3.1 Computing Randomized Encodings with the Help of Inner Products

The key insight of [LV16a] is that IPFE – currently the only collusion-resistant FE scheme based on standard assumptions – is powerful enough to indirectly compute any *constant-degree* function f (i.e. $f \in \mathbf{NC^0}$). The tool that enables this is the arithmetic RE of [AIK14], in which the computation of each element of $(\overline{f}, x)$ is linear in the bits of x and a polynomial function of some randomness r. This allows the representation of the elements of $(\overline{f}, x)$ as an inner product of some coefficient vectors (depending on f) and input vectors (depending on x), which can be computed by multiple instances of IPFE. Note that RE.Enc requires fresh (pseudo-)randomness, which cannot be provided by for example, a built-in PRG, as inner products are limited to degree-2 computation. [LV16a] resolved the problem by relying on the hardness of the jSXDH problem, which guarantees that $[ab]_{T_i}$ can be used as a source of pseudo-randomness in the presence of the encodings of $[a]_{T_i}$ and $[b]_{T_i}$ under any tag T_i.

By the nature of the existing IPFE schemes, the result of the computation (i.e. the output of decryption) still "resides in the exponent",[5] meaning that RE.Eval cannot be directly executed on the decryption outputs. This necessitates further levels of multilinearity (for IPFE, bilinear computation would be enough) to evaluate $(\overline{f}, x)$ homomorphically and to extract the binary result using the zero-test procedure of a GES.

In summary, [LV16a] have provided a method to construct secret- and, with some extra effort, public-key collusion-resistant $FE^{\mathrm{Deg}\text{-}d}$ with linear efficiency for degree-d Boolean functions using a GES with a $\kappa = 2d$ multilinearity, assuming the jSXDH assumption holds.

---

[5] Actual retrieval of the result is only possible for a polynomial-size range by testing whether the output is some specific value in the range. In pairing-based IPFE schemes, this can be tested by an exponentiation and a comparison.

6.3.2 Degree-Preserving FE

In order to further narrow the gap between the necessary multilinearity – used in bootstrappable primitives – and the standard assumption $\kappa = 2$, the next milestone was a construction of degree-preserving $FE^{Deg\text{-}d}$ from degree-d MMaps that was achieved concurrently by [Lin17] and [AS17] (see §6.4) from different assumptions.

The initial observation of [Lin17] was that, using an IPFE scheme, any quadratic function f is straightforward to compute, since it can be expressed as a linear function of quadratic monomials $f(x) = \sum_{i,j} c_{i,j} x_i x_j = \langle c, x \otimes x \rangle$. Unfortunately, the ciphertexts for $x \otimes x$ have quadratic size in $|x|$ preventing the required linear encryption time. To tackle this issue, the goal of [Lin17] was to prepare a compressed version of the ciphertext that contained just enough information for the preparation of the full ciphertext in the decryption time. For this, the compressed ciphertext must contain x and the secret key. The first idea to shorten the secret encryption key was borrowed from [LV16a] as, again relying on the DDH (and in general the SXDH) assumption, a length-$|x|^2$ random secret key s can be replaced by two length-$|x|$ ones, s' and s'', as $[s' \otimes s'']$ can provide $|x|^2$ pseudo-random values. The question now is how to securely transfer this linear-sized information (s', s'', x) needed for preparing the full ciphertext during the decryption process. The tricky idea is to nest two IPFE schemes. The inner one was based on the work of [ABCP15], because its encryption algorithm can be turned into an inner-product computation as well. Taking advantage of this, the ciphertext of the inner IPFE instance can be computed by an outer function-hiding IPFE scheme. In this way, the ciphertext of the desired quadratic FE can consist of the functional key and ciphertext (together containing (s', s'', x)) of the function-hiding outer IPFE, and decryption with these inputs results in the ciphertext of the inner [ABCP15]-based scheme, which can now be decrypted as usual.

As shown by [Lin17], this quadratic FE from bilinear maps can be generalized to $FE^{Deg\text{-}d}$ using degree-d MMaps, assuming that the SXDH assumption holds. An interesting angle on this result is that it could be implemented with the simple asymmetric MMaps of [BS03, Rot13] and does not require the more involved structure of a GES.

6.4 Realization of PAFE

Concurrently with that of [Lin17], another degree-preserving FE construction was proposed in [AS17]. Interestingly, while the implications of these results are equivalent, the approach is rather different. Most notably, the latter construction realizes related but distinct primitives using different assumptions. Namely, [AS17] obtains bootstrappable secret-key $PAFE^{Deg\text{-}d}$ from a GES with $\kappa = d$ based on a new assumption.

The approach is reminiscent of the circuit obfuscation techniques previously seen (§5.2.2): encryption is simply a bitwise GES encoding of some x, decryption is the homomorphic evaluation of some arithmetic circuit C on the encodings of x, and the recovery algorithm consists of a simple evaluation of a linear function on top-level encodings (gained from decryption) and zero-testing of the result. Of course, further countermeasures, which are extensions of previously seen techniques, are vital to circumvent the evaluation of arbitrary functions and input mixing. To prevent these, [AS17] introduced a new abstraction, called SE, which substitutes for the functionality of composite-order GESs (see §2.2.4). Furthermore, with the help of a specially structured GES (which could be based on either GGH13 or CLT13), the authors of [AS17] could also avoid the problematic additions of encodings with different tags, thus avoiding the increase in degree due to such operations.

The security argument for the resulting PAFE scheme was inspired by the so-called dual system methodology of [Wat09] and based on the AS assumption, which was proposed in the same work. The authors of [AS17] conjectured that AS can be instantiated using existing GES candidates, as it does not require the publishing of vulnerable low-level encodings of zero. While it was shown that the AS assumption is implied by the BGKPS ideal model, it is an open question whether the proposed PAFE scheme remains secure in the more challenging MSZ model as well.

Chapter 7
iO Combiners and Universal Constructions

Summarizing the results introduced in this survey, we can conclude that since the breakthrough of [GGH$^+$13b] the huge effort to better understand the nature of iO has resulted in significant progress. Instead of the "science-fiction-type" assumptions of the first candidates, currently, iO obfuscation can be based on assumptions that are closely related to standard ones. However, the validity of these assumptions is still not clear, and future work has to bridge the gap between the assumptions that imply iO and the ones that are widely accepted in cryptography. Until then, the question whether of general-purpose obfuscation is possible remains open. This kind of uncertainty is fairly frequent in cryptography, and has motivated the development of so-called combiners and universal constructions. The goal of these is to somehow reduce the uncertainty around the security of candidate realizations of a primitive. A combiner aims to integrate several candidates for the same primitive in order to achieve a new realization that is secure assuming that a subset of the candidates utilized are secure. This latter assumption is relaxed by a universal construction, which must be secure whenever the primitive in question is realizable.

We close our review by introducing obfuscation combiners and a universal construction of iO, which enhance the previously seen security features of iO candidates.

7.1 Combiners for Obfuscation

The idea of combiners dates back to the 1980s when [AB81] showed an encryption scheme, built from two others, that is at least as secure as the better one. Since then, combiners have often been used in practice (sometimes implicitly), and their formal definition was first given in [Her05, HKN$^+$05]. Informally, a standard (n, m)-combiner for a cryptographic primitive $\mathcal{P}$ is a construction that takes m correct candidate schemes for $\mathcal{P}$ and outputs a new scheme that is guaranteed to be secure

© The Author(s), under exclusive licence to Springer Nature Switzerland AG 2020
M. Horváth and L. Buttyán, *Cryptographic Obfuscation*, SpringerBriefs
in Computer Science, https://doi.org/10.1007/978-3-319-98041-6_7

provided that n of the candidates used are secure.[1] This notion is particularly useful when the candidates for $\mathcal{P}$ are based on various hardness assumptions that are not yet well understood, just as in the case of the current iO candidates. An (n,m)-combiner for $\mathcal{P}$ is called *robust* if we do not even assume the correctness of the insecure schemes, i.e. $m-n$ candidates can be faulty; if the remaining n are correct and secure, then so is the combined scheme.

Combiners for obfuscation were first investigated by [HS10], who showed that the cascade $(1,2)$-combiner for VBB obfuscation, i.e. $\mathcal{O}_2[\mathcal{O}_1[\cdot]]$, is a VBB obfuscator if both candidates maintain the functionality and slowdown requirements and one of them also fulfils the VBB security requirement of Definition 3.1. This approach is clearly not robust, as if either of the candidates were not correct functionally, then the combined scheme would be incorrect as well. On the other hand, [FHBNS16] showed a robust $(3,4)$-combiner for iO, DiO, VGB and VBB obfuscation,[2] building on the idea of the above cascade combiner. To overcome the problem mentioned above, instead of using a single (maybe corrupted) obfuscator in the first layer, three different obfuscations of a circuit C are prepared and each is executed on an input x, but only a single output is returned if a majority of the results are identical. This will be correct as long as at most one candidate is bogus. Note that the corrupted candidate could simply reveal C, but this can be hidden by a second layer of obfuscation using the fourth candidate (which still must be correct and secure). The only remaining question is how to handle the situation if the candidate in the second layer is the corrupted one. The above idea of a majority function, MAJ, can also help here if we take the majority of three different combinations of the four candidates in the structure described:

$$\text{Comb}_{\mathcal{O}_1,\mathcal{O}_2,\mathcal{O}_3,\mathcal{O}_4}(\cdot) = \text{MAJ} \begin{Bmatrix} \mathcal{O}_1(\text{MAJ}\{\mathcal{O}_2(\cdot),\mathcal{O}_3(\cdot),\mathcal{O}_4(\cdot)\}), \\ \mathcal{O}_2(\text{MAJ}\{\mathcal{O}_1(\cdot),\mathcal{O}_3(\cdot),\mathcal{O}_4(\cdot)\}), \\ \mathcal{O}_3(\text{MAJ}\{\mathcal{O}_1(\cdot),\mathcal{O}_2(\cdot),\mathcal{O}_4(\cdot)\}) \end{Bmatrix}.$$

On the negative side, [FHBNS16] proved the impossibility of structural $(2,3)$-combiners, where "structural" means that the combined scheme relies only on the candidate obfuscators and no other primitives.[3]

The non-structural paradigm was investigated by [AJN+16, AJS17a], who proposed robust $(1,n)$-combiners for iO under different assumptions. [AJN+16] assumed the (sub-exponential) hardness of either the DDH or the LWE problem and the (sub-exponential) security of one of n iO candidates. To see the intuition behind their solution (based on LWE), first suppose that all n candidates are correct. Unlike the case of structural combiners, none of the candidates has direct access to the input circuit C, but each one is used to obfuscate an individual puzzle piece of the

---

[1] We note that the combined scheme has to run in time polynomial in m, the security parameter, and the input length of $\mathcal{P}$ (naturally, the candidates used are also assumed to run in polynomial-time).

[2] Note that the negative results for some of these notions do not rule out the possibility that for some specific functionalities there exist obfuscators fulfilling these definitions; thus, combining them is also meaningful.

[3] We note that these two results were generalized in [FHBNS16] to $(2\gamma+1,3\gamma+1)$- and $(2\gamma,3\gamma)$-combiners, respectively, for any constant γ.

computation of $C(x)$. The outputs of these pieces can then be combined together to reveal the value of $C(x)$. The underlying primitive which helps to realize this is the threshold multi-key FHE scheme of [MW16]. This primitive allowed the authors of [AJN$^+$16] to argue that until a single obfuscator candidate hides a "secret-share" of the computation, circuit C remains hidden and thus the combined iO scheme is secure. Robustness can be achieved by cleverly building on the transformation of [BV16], which turns an approximately correct iO scheme into a perfectly correct one. [AJS17a] improved this result by relaxing the necessary assumption to the existence of (sub-exponentially secure) OWFs.

7.2 Universal iO

While in §7.1 we introduced a concept that also has practical significance (see the implementation of [FHBNS16]), we now turn our attention to a related but highly theoretical notion. We have seen that a $(1,k)$-robust combiner for $\mathcal{P}$ securely realizes $\mathcal{P}$ if any candidate from a set of k candidates securely realizes $\mathcal{P}$. The definition of a *universal construction* for $\mathcal{P}$ takes a step even further in relaxing the requirement for providing a secure realization of $\mathcal{P}$. Namely, it does not require that a secure candidate has to be contained in an explicit list (and thus we already have to know about it), but only that there exists a secure candidate. In other words, a universal scheme for $\mathcal{P}$ is an explicit method to securely realize $\mathcal{P}$ if it is not impossible to securely realize $\mathcal{P}$ (for more details of these definitions and their relations, see [HKN$^+$05]). Notice the interesting implications of the definition, particularly that the only way to break a universal construction is to prove that no other scheme can securely realize $\mathcal{P}$ either. Also, observe that such schemes automatically turn any non-constructive possibility results for $\mathcal{P}$ into a concrete realization even if the significance of such a realization is rather theoretical. If we now substitute $\mathcal{P}$ with iO, we see that a universal iO construction would have these very attractive features; this was first observed by [GK16]. Using a similar approach to the universal OWF construction of Levin [Lev87], [AJN$^+$16] showed that a $(1,k)$-robust iO combiner for arbitrary k implies a universal iO scheme. Their result states that if the LWE assumption holds and the notion of indistinguishability obfuscation is possible to realize securely, then their universal iO candidate is a secure obfuscator.

References

[5GE] 5gen framework. https://github.com/5GenCrypto, Accessed 20 Dec. 2017.

[Aar05] Scott Aaronson. Ten semi-grand challenges for quantum computing theory, 2005. http://www.scottaaronson.com/writings/qchallenge.html, Accessed 20 Dec. 2017.

[AB81] C.A. Asmuth and G.R. Blakley. An efficient algorithm for constructing a cryptosystem which is harder to break than two other cryptosystems. *Computers & Mathematics with Applications*, 7(6):447–450, 1981.

[AB15] Benny Applebaum and Zvika Brakerski. Obfuscating circuits via composite-order graded encoding. In Yevgeniy Dodis and Jesper Buus Nielsen, editors, *Theory of Cryptography - 12th Theory of Cryptography Conference, TCC 2015, Warsaw, Poland, March 23-25, 2015, Proceedings, Part II*, volume 9015 of *Lecture Notes in Computer Science*, pages 528–556. Springer, 2015.

[ABC+15] Frederik Armknecht, Colin Boyd, Christopher Carr, Kristian Gjøsteen, Angela Jäschke, Christian A. Reuter, and Martin Strand. A guide to fully homomorphic encryption. Cryptology ePrint Archive, Report 2015/1192, 2015. http://eprint.iacr.org/2015/1192, Version: 20160914:161519.

[ABCP15] Michel Abdalla, Florian Bourse, Angelo De Caro, and David Pointcheval. Simple functional encryption schemes for inner products. In Jonathan Katz, editor, *Public-Key Cryptography - PKC 2015 - 18th IACR International Conference on Practice and Theory in Public-Key Cryptography, Gaithersburg, MD, USA, March 30 - April 1, 2015, Proceedings*, volume 9020 of *Lecture Notes in Computer Science*, pages 733–751. Springer, 2015.

[ABD16] Martin R. Albrecht, Shi Bai, and Léo Ducas. A subfield lattice attack on overstretched NTRU assumptions - cryptanalysis of some FHE and graded encoding schemes. In *Advances in Cryptology - CRYPTO 2016 - 36th Annual International Cryptology Conference, Santa Barbara,*

© The Author(s), under exclusive licence to Springer Nature Switzerland AG 2020
M. Horváth and L. Buttyán, *Cryptographic Obfuscation*, SpringerBriefs
in Computer Science, https://doi.org/10.1007/978-3-319-98041-6

CA, USA, August 14-18, 2016, Proceedings, Part I, pages 153–178, 2016.

[ABG+13] Prabhanjan Ananth, Dan Boneh, Sanjam Garg, Amit Sahai, and Mark Zhandry. Differing-inputs obfuscation and applications. Cryptology ePrint Archive, Report 2013/689, 2013. https://eprint.iacr.org/2013/689, Version: 20140617:013344.

[ABSV15] Prabhanjan Ananth, Zvika Brakerski, Gil Segev, and Vinod Vaikuntanathan. From selective to adaptive security in functional encryption. In Rosario Gennaro and Matthew Robshaw, editors, *Advances in Cryptology - CRYPTO 2015 - 35th Annual Cryptology Conference, Santa Barbara, CA, USA, August 16-20, 2015, Proceedings, Part II*, volume 9216 of *Lecture Notes in Computer Science*, pages 657–677. Springer, 2015.

[ACLL15] Martin R. Albrecht, Catalin Cocis, Fabien Laguillaumie, and Adeline Langlois. Implementing candidate graded encoding schemes from ideal lattices. In *Advances in Cryptology - ASIACRYPT 2015 - 21st International Conference on the Theory and Application of Cryptology and Information Security, Auckland, New Zealand, November 29 - December 3, 2015, Proceedings, Part II*, pages 752–775, 2015.

[AD] Martin R. Albrecht and Alex Davidson. Are graded encoding scheme broken yet? http://malb.io/are-graded-encoding-schemes-broken-yet.html, Accessed: 20 Dec. 2017.

[ADGM17] Daniel Apon, Nico Döttling, Sanjam Garg, and Pratyay Mukherjee. Cryptanalysis of indistinguishability obfuscations of circuits over GGH13. In Ioannis Chatzigiannakis, Piotr Indyk, Fabian Kuhn, and Anca Muscholl, editors, *44th International Colloquium on Automata, Languages, and Programming, ICALP 2017, July 10-14, 2017, Warsaw, Poland*, volume 80 of *LIPIcs*, pages 38:1–38:16. Schloss Dagstuhl - Leibniz-Zentrum fuer Informatik, 2017.

[AF16] Gorjan Alagic and Bill Fefferman. On quantum obfuscation, 2016. Talk at QCrypt, available at arXiv:1602.01771.

[AFH+15] Martin R. Albrecht, Pooya Farshim, Shuai Han, Dennis Hofheinz, Enrique Larraia, and Kenneth G. Paterson. Multilinear maps from obfuscation. Cryptology ePrint Archive, Report 2015/780, 2015. https://eprint.iacr.org/2015/780, Version: 20171218:145841.

[AFH+16] Martin R. Albrecht, Pooya Farshim, Dennis Hofheinz, Enrique Larraia, and Kenneth G. Paterson. Multilinear maps from obfuscation. In *Theory of Cryptography - 13th International Conference, TCC 2016-A, Tel Aviv, Israel, January 10-13, 2016, Proceedings, Part I*, pages 446–473, 2016.

[AGIS14] Prabhanjan Ananth, Divya Gupta, Yuval Ishai, and Amit Sahai. Optimizing Obfuscation: Avoiding Barrington's Theorem. In *Proceedings of the 2014 ACM SIGSAC Conference on Computer and Communications Security*, pages 646–658. ACM, 2014.

[Agr18] Shweta Agrawal. New methods for indistinguishability obfuscation: Bootstrapping and instantiation. Cryptology ePrint Archive, Report 2018/633, 2018. https://eprint.iacr.org/2018/633 Version:20180626:160513.

[AGVW13] Shweta Agrawal, Sergey Gorbunov, Vinod Vaikuntanathan, and Hoeteck Wee. Functional encryption: New perspectives and lower bounds. In *Advances in Cryptology - CRYPTO 2013 - 33rd Annual Cryptology Conference, Santa Barbara, CA, USA, August 18-22, 2013. Proceedings, Part II*, pages 500–518, 2013.

[AHKM14] Daniel Apon, Yan Huang, Jonathan Katz, and Alex J. Malozemoff. Implementing cryptographic program obfuscation. Cryptology ePrint Archive, Report 2014/779 (Crypto-2014 Rump Session), 2014. https://eprint.iacr.org/2014/779, Version: 20150210:203741.

[AIK04] Benny Applebaum, Yuval Ishai, and Eyal Kushilevitz. Cryptography in NC^0. In *45th Symposium on Foundations of Computer Science (FOCS 2004), 17-19 October 2004, Rome, Italy, Proceedings*, pages 166–175, 2004.

[AIK06] Benny Applebaum, Yuval Ishai, and Eyal Kushilevitz. Computationally private randomizing polynomials and their applications. *Computational Complexity*, 15(2):115–162, 2006.

[AIK14] Benny Applebaum, Yuval Ishai, and Eyal Kushilevitz. How to garble arithmetic circuits. *SIAM J. Comput.*, 43(2):905–929, 2014.

[AJ15] Prabhanjan Ananth and Abhishek Jain. Indistinguishability obfuscation from compact functional encryption. In *Advances in Cryptology - CRYPTO 2015 - 35th Annual Cryptology Conference, Santa Barbara, CA, USA, August 16-20, 2015, Proceedings, Part I*, pages 308–326, 2015.

[AJN+16] Prabhanjan Ananth, Aayush Jain, Moni Naor, Amit Sahai, and Eylon Yogev. Universal constructions and robust combiners for indistinguishability obfuscation and witness encryption. In *Advances in Cryptology - CRYPTO 2016 - 36th Annual International Cryptology Conference, Santa Barbara, CA, USA, August 14-18, 2016, Proceedings, Part II*, pages 491–520, 2016.

[AJS15] Prabhanjan Ananth, Abhishek Jain, and Amit Sahai. Indistinguishability obfuscation from functional encryption for simple functions. Cryptology ePrint Archive, Report 2015/730, 2015. https://eprint.iacr.org/2015/730, Version: 20151028:184618.

[AJS17a] Prabhanjan Ananth, Aayush Jain, and Amit Sahai. Robust transforming combiners from indistinguishability obfuscation to functional encryption. In *Advances in Cryptology - EUROCRYPT 2017 - 36th Annual International Conference on the Theory and Applications of Cryptographic Techniques, Paris, France, April 30 - May 4, 2017, Proceedings, Part I*, pages 91–121, 2017.

[AJS17b] Prabhanjan Ananth, Abhishek Jain, and Amit Sahai. Indistinguisha-bility obfuscation for Turing machines: Constant overhead and amor-tization. In Jonathan Katz and Hovav Shacham, editors, *Advances in Cryptology - CRYPTO 2017 - 37th Annual International Cryptology Conference, Santa Barbara, CA, USA, August 20-24, 2017, Proceed-ings, Part II*, volume 10402 of *Lecture Notes in Computer Science*, pages 252–279. Springer, 2017.

[AJS18] Prabhanjan Ananth, Aayush Jain, and Amit Sahai. Indistinguisha-bility obfuscation without multilinear maps: iO from LWE, bilinear maps, and weak pseudorandomness. Cryptology ePrint Archive, Re-port 2018/615, 2018. https://eprint.iacr.org/2018/615 Ver-sion:20180622:144801.

[AKG17] Scott Aaronson, Greg Kuperberg, and Christopher Granade. Com-plexity Zoo, 2017. https://complexityzoo.uwaterloo.ca/, Ac-cessed 20 Dec. 2017.

[Ama] Amazon Web Services. https://aws.amazon.com/amazon-ai/, Accessed 20 Dec. 2017.

[And08] W. Erik Anderson. On the secure obfuscation of deterministic finite automata. Cryptology ePrint Archive, Report 2008/184, 2008. http://eprint.iacr.org/2008/184, Version: 20080602:143730.

[App14a] Benny Applebaum. Bootstrapping obfuscators via fast pseudorandom functions. In *Advances in Cryptology - ASIACRYPT 2014 - 20th In-ternational Conference on the Theory and Application of Cryptology and Information Security, Kaoshiung, Taiwan, R.O.C., December 7-11, 2014, Proceedings, Part II*, pages 162–172, 2014.

[App14b] Benny Applebaum. *Cryptography in Constant Parallel Time*. Infor-mation Security and Cryptography. Springer, 2014.

[App16] Benny Applebaum. Cryptographic hardness of random local functions – survey. *Computational Complexity*, 25(3):667–722, 2016.

[App17] Benny Applebaum. Garbled circuits as randomized encodings of func-tions: a primer. In Yehuda Lindell, editor, *Tutorials on the Foundations of Cryptography*, pages 1–44. Springer International Publishing, 2017.

[AS17] Prabhanjan Ananth and Amit Sahai. Projective arithmetic functional encryption and indistinguishability obfuscation from degree-5 multi-linear maps. In Jean-Sébastien Coron and Jesper Buus Nielsen, ed-itors, *Advances in Cryptology - EUROCRYPT 2017 - 36th Annual International Conference on the Theory and Applications of Crypto-graphic Techniques, Paris, France, April 30 - May 4, 2017, Proceed-ings, Part I*, volume 10210 of *Lecture Notes in Computer Science*, pages 152–181, 2017.

[AW07] Ben Adida and Douglas Wikström. How to shuffle in public. In *The-ory of Cryptography, 4th Theory of Cryptography Conference, TCC 2007, Amsterdam, The Netherlands, February 21-24, 2007, Proceed-ings*, pages 555–574, 2007.

[Bar86]   David A. Barrington. Bounded-width polynomial-size branching programs recognize exactly those languages in NC^1. In Juris Hartmanis, editor, *Proceedings of the 18th Annual ACM Symposium on Theory of Computing, May 28-30, 1986, Berkeley, California, USA*, pages 1–5. ACM, 1986.

[Bar16a]   Boaz Barak. Hopes, fears, and software obfuscation. *Commun. ACM*, 59(3):88–96, February 2016.

[Bar16b]   Boaz Barak. Lecture notes from the Cryptography course at Harvard University, Spring 2016. https://intensecrypto.org/public/lec_17_SFE.html, Accessed 16 July 2019.

[BBF13]   Paul Baecher, Christina Brzuska, and Marc Fischlin. Notions of black-box reductions, revisited. In *Advances in Cryptology - ASIACRYPT 2013 - 19th International Conference on the Theory and Application of Cryptology and Information Security, Bengaluru, India, December 1-5, 2013, Proceedings, Part I*, pages 296–315, 2013.

[BBKK17]   Boaz Barak, Zvika Brakerski, Ilan Komargodski, and Pravesh Kothari. Limits on low-degree pseudorandom generators (or: Sum-of-squares meets program obfuscation). *Electronic Colloquium on Computational Complexity (ECCC)*, 24:60, 2017.

[BC14]   Nir Bitansky and Ran Canetti. On strong simulation and composable point obfuscation. *Journal of Cryptology*, 27(2):317–357, 2014.

[BCC⁺14]   Nir Bitansky, Ran Canetti, Henry Cohn, Shafi Goldwasser, Yael Tauman Kalai, Omer Paneth, and Alon Rosen. The impossibility of obfuscation with auxiliary input or a universal simulator. In *Advances in Cryptology - CRYPTO 2014 - 34th Annual Cryptology Conference, Santa Barbara, CA, USA, August 17-21, 2014, Proceedings, Part II*, pages 71–89, 2014.

[BCC⁺17]   Nir Bitansky, Ran Canetti, Alessandro Chiesa, Shafi Goldwasser, Huijia Lin, Aviad Rubinstein, and Eran Tromer. The hunting of the SNARK. *Journal of Cryptology*, 30(4):989–1066, 2017.

[BCG⁺11]   Nir Bitansky, Ran Canetti, Shafi Goldwasser, Shai Halevi, Yael Tauman Kalai, and Guy N Rothblum. Program obfuscation with leaky hardware. In *Advances in Cryptology-ASIACRYPT 2011*, pages 722–739. Springer, 2011.

[BCKP14]   Nir Bitansky, Ran Canetti, Yael Tauman Kalai, and Omer Paneth. On virtual grey box obfuscation for general circuits. In *Advances in Cryptology - CRYPTO 2014 - 34th Annual Cryptology Conference, Santa Barbara, CA, USA, August 17-21, 2014, Proceedings, Part II*, pages 108–125, 2014.

[BCP14]   Elette Boyle, Kai-Min Chung, and Rafael Pass. On extractability obfuscation. In Yehuda Lindell, editor, *Theory of Cryptography - 11th Theory of Cryptography Conference, TCC 2014, San Diego, CA, USA, February 24-26, 2014. Proceedings*, volume 8349 of *Lecture Notes in Computer Science*, pages 52–73. Springer, 2014.

[BD16] Zvika Brakerski and Or Dagmi. Shorter circuit obfuscation in challenging security models. In *Security and Cryptography for Networks - 10th International Conference, SCN 2016, Amalfi, Italy, August 31 - September 2, 2016, Proceedings*, pages 551–570, 2016.

[BGH⁺15] Zvika Brakerski, Craig Gentry, Shai Halevi, Tancrède Lepoint, Amit Sahai, and Mehdi Tibouchi. Cryptanalysis of the quadratic zero-testing of GGH. Cryptology ePrint Archive, Report 2015/845, 2015. https://eprint.iacr.org/2015/845, Version: 20150901:231544.

[BGI⁺01] Boaz Barak, Oded Goldreich, Russell Impagliazzo, Steven Rudich, Amit Sahai, Salil P. Vadhan, and Ke Yang. On the (im)possibility of obfuscating programs. In Joe Kilian, editor, *Advances in Cryptology - CRYPTO 2001, 21st Annual International Cryptology Conference, Santa Barbara, California, USA, August 19-23, 2001, Proceedings*, volume 2139 of *Lecture Notes in Computer Science*, pages 1–18. Springer, 2001.

[BGI⁺12] Boaz Barak, Oded Goldreich, Russell Impagliazzo, Steven Rudich, Amit Sahai, Salil P. Vadhan, and Ke Yang. On the (im)possibility of obfuscating programs. *Journal of the ACM*, 59(2):6:1–6:48, 2012.

[BGI⁺14a] Amos Beimel, Ariel Gabizon, Yuval Ishai, Eyal Kushilevitz, Sigurd Meldgaard, and Anat Paskin-Cherniavsky. Non-interactive secure multiparty computation. In Juan A. Garay and Rosario Gennaro, editors, *Advances in Cryptology - CRYPTO 2014 - 34th Annual Cryptology Conference, Santa Barbara, CA, USA, August 17-21, 2014, Proceedings, Part II*, volume 8617 of *Lecture Notes in Computer Science*, pages 387–404. Springer, 2014.

[BGI14b] Elette Boyle, Shafi Goldwasser, and Ioana Ivan. Functional signatures and pseudorandom functions. In *Public-Key Cryptography - PKC 2014 - 17th International Conference on Practice and Theory in Public-Key Cryptography, Buenos Aires, Argentina, March 26-28, 2014. Proceedings*, pages 501–519, 2014.

[BGK⁺14] Boaz Barak, Sanjam Garg, Yael Tauman Kalai, Omer Paneth, and Amit Sahai. Protecting obfuscation against algebraic attacks. In *Advances in Cryptology–EUROCRYPT 2014*, pages 221–238. Springer, 2014.

[BGL⁺15] Nir Bitansky, Sanjam Garg, Huijia Lin, Rafael Pass, and Sidharth Telang. Succinct randomized encodings and their applications. In *Proceedings of the Forty-Seventh Annual ACM on Symposium on Theory of Computing*, STOC '15, pages 439–448, New York, NY, USA, 2015. ACM. Full version: http://eprint.iacr.org/2015/356.

[BGN05] Dan Boneh, Eu-Jin Goh, and Kobbi Nissim. Evaluating 2-DNF formulas on ciphertexts. In *Theory of Cryptography, Second Theory of Cryptography Conference, TCC 2005, Cambridge, MA, USA, February 10-12, 2005, Proceedings*, pages 325–341, 2005.

[BHLN15] Daniel J. Bernstein, Andreas Hülsing, Tanja Lange, and Ruben Niederhagen. Bad directions in cryptographic hash functions. In Ernest

Foo and Douglas Stebila, editors, *Information Security and Privacy - 20th Australasian Conference, ACISP 2015, Brisbane, QLD, Australia, June 29 - July 1, 2015, Proceedings*, volume 9144 of *Lecture Notes in Computer Science*, pages 488–508. Springer, 2015.

[BHMT16] Joppe W. Bos, Charles Hubain, Wil Michiels, and Philippe Teuwen. Differential computation analysis: Hiding your white-box designs is not enough. In Benedikt Gierlichs and Axel Y. Poschmann, editors, *Cryptographic Hardware and Embedded Systems - CHES 2016 - 18th International Conference, Santa Barbara, CA, USA, August 17-19, 2016, Proceedings*, volume 9813 of *Lecture Notes in Computer Science*, pages 215–236. Springer, 2016.

[Big] BigML. https://bigml.com/ Accessed 20 Dec 2017.

[BISW17] Dan Boneh, Yuval Ishai, Amit Sahai, and David J. Wu. Lattice-based snargs and their application to more efficient obfuscation. In *Advances in Cryptology - EUROCRYPT 2017 - 36th Annual International Conference on the Theory and Applications of Cryptographic Techniques, Paris, France, April 30 - May 4, 2017, Proceedings, Part III*, pages 247–277, 2017.

[BJK15] Allison Bishop, Abhishek Jain, and Lucas Kowalczyk. Function-hiding inner product encryption. In *Advances in Cryptology - ASIACRYPT 2015 - 21st International Conference on the Theory and Application of Cryptology and Information Security, Auckland, New Zealand, November 29 - December 3, 2015, Proceedings, Part I*, pages 470–491, 2015.

[BKS16] Zvika Brakerski, Ilan Komargodski, and Gil Segev. Multi-input functional encryption in the private-key setting: Stronger security from weaker assumptions. In Marc Fischlin and Jean-Sébastien Coron, editors, *Advances in Cryptology - EUROCRYPT 2016 - 35th Annual International Conference on the Theory and Applications of Cryptographic Techniques, Vienna, Austria, May 8-12, 2016, Proceedings, Part II*, volume 9666 of *Lecture Notes in Computer Science*, pages 852–880. Springer, 2016.

[BLMR13] Dan Boneh, Kevin Lewi, Hart William Montgomery, and Ananth Raghunathan. Key homomorphic PRFs and their applications. In Ran Canetti and Juan A. Garay, editors, *Advances in Cryptology - CRYPTO 2013 - 33rd Annual Cryptology Conference, Santa Barbara, CA, USA, August 18-22, 2013. Proceedings, Part I*, volume 8042 of *Lecture Notes in Computer Science*, pages 410–428. Springer, 2013.

[BLR+15] Dan Boneh, Kevin Lewi, Mariana Raykova, Amit Sahai, Mark Zhandry, and Joe Zimmerman. Semantically secure order-revealing encryption: Multi-input functional encryption without obfuscation. In *Advances in Cryptology - EUROCRYPT 2015 - 34th Annual International Conference on the Theory and Applications of Cryptographic Techniques, Sofia, Bulgaria, April 26-30, 2015, Proceedings, Part II*, pages 563–594, 2015.

[BMSZ16] Saikrishna Badrinarayanan, Eric Miles, Amit Sahai, and Mark Zhandry. Post-zeroizing obfuscation: New mathematical tools, and the case of evasive circuits. In Marc Fischlin and Jean-Sébastien Coron, editors, *Advances in Cryptology - EUROCRYPT 2016 - 35th Annual International Conference on the Theory and Applications of Cryptographic Techniques, Vienna, Austria, May 8-12, 2016, Proceedings, Part II*, volume 9666 of *Lecture Notes in Computer Science*, pages 764–791. Springer, 2016.

[BNPW16] Nir Bitansky, Ryo Nishimaki, Alain Passelègue, and Daniel Wichs. From cryptomania to obfustopia through secret-key functional encryption. In Martin Hirt and Adam D. Smith, editors, *Theory of Cryptography - 14th International Conference, TCC 2016-B, Beijing, China, October 31 - November 3, 2016, Proceedings, Part II*, volume 9986 of *Lecture Notes in Computer Science*, pages 391–418, 2016.

[BOKP15] Sebastian Banescu, Martín Ochoa, Nils Kunze, and Alexander Pretschner. Idea: Benchmarking indistinguishability obfuscation - A candidate implementation. In *Engineering Secure Software and Systems - 7th International Symposium, ESSoS 2015, Milan, Italy, March 4-6, 2015. Proceedings*, pages 149–156, 2015.

[BP13] Nir Bitansky and Omer Paneth. On the impossibility of approximate obfuscation and applications to resettable cryptography. In Dan Boneh, Tim Roughgarden, and Joan Feigenbaum, editors, *Symposium on Theory of Computing Conference, STOC'13, Palo Alto, CA, USA, June 1-4, 2013*, pages 241–250. ACM, 2013.

[BP15] Elette Boyle and Rafael Pass. Limits of extractability assumptions with distributional auxiliary input. In *Advances in Cryptology - ASIACRYPT 2015 - 21st International Conference on the Theory and Application of Cryptology and Information Security, Auckland, New Zealand, November 29 - December 3, 2015, Proceedings, Part II*, pages 236–261, 2015.

[BR93] Mihir Bellare and Phillip Rogaway. Random oracles are practical: A paradigm for designing efficient protocols. In *CCS '93, Proceedings of the 1st ACM Conference on Computer and Communications Security, Fairfax, Virginia, USA, November 3-5, 1993.*, pages 62–73, 1993.

[BR13] Zvika Brakerski and Guy N. Rothblum. Obfuscating conjunctions. In *Advances in Cryptology - CRYPTO 2013 - 33rd Annual Cryptology Conference, Santa Barbara, CA, USA, August 18-22, 2013. Proceedings, Part II*, pages 416–434, 2013.

[BR14a] Zvika Brakerski and Guy N. Rothblum. Black-box obfuscation for d-CNFs. In Moni Naor, editor, *Innovations in Theoretical Computer Science, ITCS'14, Princeton, NJ, USA, January 12-14, 2014*, pages 235–250. ACM, 2014.

[BR14b] Zvika Brakerski and Guy N. Rothblum. Virtual black-box obfuscation for all circuits via generic graded encoding. In Yehuda Lindell, editor, *Theory of Cryptography - 11th Theory of Cryptography Con-

ference, TCC 2014, San Diego, CA, USA, February 24-26, 2014. Proceedings, volume 8349 of *Lecture Notes in Computer Science*, pages 1–25. Springer, 2014.

[BS03] Dan Boneh and Alice Silverberg. Applications of multilinear forms to cryptography. *Contemporary Mathematics*, 324(1):71–90, 2003.

[BS15] Zvika Brakerski and Gil Segev. Function-private functional encryption in the private-key setting. In *Theory of Cryptography - 12th Theory of Cryptography Conference, TCC 2015, Warsaw, Poland, March 23-25, 2015, Proceedings, Part II*, pages 306–324, 2015.

[BST14] Mihir Bellare, Igors Stepanovs, and Stefano Tessaro. Poly-many hardcore bits for any one-way function and a framework for differing-inputs obfuscation. In *Advances in Cryptology - ASIACRYPT 2014 - 20th International Conference on the Theory and Application of Cryptology and Information Security, Kaoshiung, Taiwan, R.O.C., December 7-11, 2014, Proceedings, Part II*, pages 102–121, 2014.

[BSW11] Dan Boneh, Amit Sahai, and Brent Waters. Functional encryption: Definitions and challenges. In Yuval Ishai, editor, *Theory of Cryptography - 8th Theory of Cryptography Conference, TCC 2011, Providence, RI, USA, March 28-30, 2011. Proceedings*, volume 6597 of *Lecture Notes in Computer Science*, pages 253–273. Springer, 2011.

[BSW16] Mihir Bellare, Igors Stepanovs, and Brent Waters. New negative results on differing-inputs obfuscation. In Marc Fischlin and Jean-Sébastien Coron, editors, *Advances in Cryptology - EUROCRYPT 2016 - 35th Annual International Conference on the Theory and Applications of Cryptographic Techniques, Vienna, Austria, May 8-12, 2016, Proceedings, Part II*, volume 9666 of *Lecture Notes in Computer Science*, pages 792–821. Springer, 2016.

[BV15] Nir Bitansky and Vinod Vaikuntanathan. Indistinguishability obfuscation from functional encryption. In *IEEE 56th Annual Symposium on Foundations of Computer Science, FOCS 2015, Berkeley, CA, USA, 17-20 October, 2015*, pages 171–190, 2015.

[BV16] Nir Bitansky and Vinod Vaikuntanathan. Indistinguishability obfuscation: From approximate to exact. In *Theory of Cryptography - 13th International Conference, TCC 2016-A, Tel Aviv, Israel, January 10-13, 2016, Proceedings, Part I*, pages 67–95, 2016.

[BW13] Dan Boneh and Brent Waters. Constrained pseudorandom functions and their applications. In *Advances in Cryptology - ASIACRYPT 2013 - 19th International Conference on the Theory and Application of Cryptology and Information Security, Bengaluru, India, December 1-5, 2013, Proceedings, Part II*, pages 280–300, 2013.

[BWZ14] Dan Boneh, David J. Wu, and Joe Zimmerman. Immunizing multilinear maps against zeroizing attacks. Cryptology ePrint Archive, Report 2014/930, 2014. https://eprint.iacr.org/2014/930, Version: 20150526:032033.

[Can97] Ran Canetti. Towards realizing random oracles: Hash functions that hide all partial information. In *Advances in Cryptology - CRYPTO '97, 17th Annual International Cryptology Conference, Santa Barbara, California, USA, August 17-21, 1997, Proceedings*, pages 455–469, 1997.

[Can15] Ran Canetti. Indistinguishability obfuscation and multi-linear maps: A brave new world, July 6 2015. https://bit.ly/2KIImAp, Accessed 20 Dec. 2017.

[CCK⁺13] Jung Hee Cheon, Jean-Sébastien Coron, Jinsu Kim, Moon Sung Lee, Tancrède Lepoint, Mehdi Tibouchi, and Aaram Yun. Batch fully homomorphic encryption over the integers. In Thomas Johansson and Phong Q. Nguyen, editors, *Advances in Cryptology - EUROCRYPT 2013, 32nd Annual International Conference on the Theory and Applications of Cryptographic Techniques, Athens, Greece, May 26-30, 2013. Proceedings*, volume 7881 of *Lecture Notes in Computer Science*, pages 315–335. Springer, 2013.

[CEJvO02] Stanley Chow, Philip A. Eisen, Harold Johnson, and Paul C. van Oorschot. A white-box DES implementation for DRM applications. In *Security and Privacy in Digital Rights Management, ACM CCS-9 Workshop, DRM 2002, Washington, DC, USA, November 18, 2002, Revised Papers*, pages 1–15, 2002.

[CFL⁺16] Jung Hee Cheon, Pierre-Alain Fouque, Changmin Lee, Brice Minaud, and Hansol Ryu. Cryptanalysis of the new CLT multilinear map over the integers. In Marc Fischlin and Jean-Sébastien Coron, editors, *Advances in Cryptology - EUROCRYPT 2016 - 35th Annual International Conference on the Theory and Applications of Cryptographic Techniques, Vienna, Austria, May 8-12, 2016, Proceedings, Part I*, volume 9665 of *Lecture Notes in Computer Science*, pages 509–536. Springer, 2016.

[CGH04] Ran Canetti, Oded Goldreich, and Shai Halevi. The random oracle methodology, revisited. *Journal of the ACM*, 51(4):557–594, 2004.

[CGH⁺15] Jean-Sébastien Coron, Craig Gentry, Shai Halevi, Tancrède Lepoint, Hemanta K. Maji, Eric Miles, Mariana Raykova, Amit Sahai, and Mehdi Tibouchi. Zeroizing without low-level zeroes: New MMAP attacks and their limitations. In Rosario Gennaro and Matthew Robshaw, editors, *Advances in Cryptology - CRYPTO 2015 - 35th Annual Cryptology Conference, Santa Barbara, CA, USA, August 16-20, 2015, Proceedings, Part I*, volume 9215 of *Lecture Notes in Computer Science*, pages 247–266. Springer, 2015.

[CGH17] Yilei Chen, Craig Gentry, and Shai Halevi. Cryptanalyses of candidate branching program obfuscators. In *Advances in Cryptology - EUROCRYPT 2017 - 36th Annual International Conference on the Theory and Applications of Cryptographic Techniques, Paris, France, April 30 - May 4, 2017, Proceedings, Part III*, pages 278–307, 2017.

[CGP15] Ran Canetti, Shafi Goldwasser, and Oxana Poburinnaya. Adaptively secure two-party computation from indistinguishability obfuscation. In Yevgeniy Dodis and Jesper Buus Nielsen, editors, *Theory of Cryptography - 12th Theory of Cryptography Conference, TCC 2015, Warsaw, Poland, March 23-25, 2015, Proceedings, Part II*, volume 9015 of *Lecture Notes in Computer Science*, pages 557–585. Springer, 2015.

[Che16] Yilei Chen. An alternative view of the graph-induced multilinear maps. Cryptology ePrint Archive, Report 2016/200, 2016. http://eprint.iacr.org/2016/200, Version: 20160301:125529.

[CHJV14] Ran Canetti, Justin Holmgren, Abhishek Jain, and Vinod Vaikuntanathan. Indistinguishability obfuscation of iterated circuits and RAM programs. Cryptology ePrint Archive, Report 2014/769, 2014. http://eprint.iacr.org/2014/769, Version: 20140930:124723.

[CHL+15] Jung Hee Cheon, Kyoohyung Han, Changmin Lee, Hansol Ryu, and Damien Stehlé. Cryptanalysis of the multilinear map over the integers. In *Advances in Cryptology - EUROCRYPT 2015 - 34th Annual International Conference on the Theory and Applications of Cryptographic Techniques, Sofia, Bulgaria, April 26-30, 2015, Proceedings, Part I*, pages 3–12, 2015.

[CJL16] Jung Hee Cheon, Jinhyuck Jeong, and Changmin Lee. An algorithm for NTRU problems and cryptanalysis of the GGH multilinear map without a low-level encoding of zero. *LMS Journal of Computation and Mathematics*, 19(A):255–266, 2016.

[CKP15] Ran Canetti, Yael Tauman Kalai, and Omer Paneth. On obfuscation with random oracles. In *Theory of Cryptography - 12th Theory of Cryptography Conference, TCC 2015, Warsaw, Poland, March 23-25, 2015, Proceedings, Part II*, pages 456–467, 2015.

[CLLT16] Jean-Sébastien Coron, Moon Sung Lee, Tancrède Lepoint, and Mehdi Tibouchi. Cryptanalysis of GGH15 multilinear maps. In *Advances in Cryptology - CRYPTO 2016 - 36th Annual International Cryptology Conference, Santa Barbara, CA, USA, August 14-18, 2016, Proceedings, Part II*, pages 607–628, 2016.

[CLLT17] Jean-Sébastien Coron, Moon Sung Lee, Tancrède Lepoint, and Mehdi Tibouchi. Zeroizing attacks on indistinguishability obfuscation over CLT13. In Serge Fehr, editor, *Public-Key Cryptography - PKC 2017 - 20th IACR International Conference on Practice and Theory in Public-Key Cryptography, Amsterdam, The Netherlands, March 28-31, 2017, Proceedings, Part I*, volume 10174 of *Lecture Notes in Computer Science*, pages 41–58. Springer, 2017.

[CLT13] Jean-Sébastien Coron, Tancrède Lepoint, and Mehdi Tibouchi. Practical multilinear maps over the integers. In *Advances in Cryptology– CRYPTO 2013*, pages 476–493. Springer, 2013.

[CLT15] Jean-Sébastien Coron, Tancrède Lepoint, and Mehdi Tibouchi. New multilinear maps over the integers. In *Advances in Cryptology - CRYPTO 2015 - 35th Annual Cryptology Conference, Santa Barbara,*

CA, USA, August 16-20, 2015, Proceedings, Part I, pages 267–286, 2015.

[CLTV15] Ran Canetti, Huijia Lin, Stefano Tessaro, and Vinod Vaikuntanathan. Obfuscation of probabilistic circuits and applications. In *Theory of Cryptography - 12th Theory of Cryptography Conference, TCC 2015, Warsaw, Poland, March 23-25, 2015, Proceedings, Part II*, pages 468–497, 2015.

[CMR17] Brent Carmer, Alex J. Malozemoff, and Mariana Raykova. 5Gen-C: Multi-input functional encryption and program obfuscation for arithmetic circuits. In Bhavani M. Thuraisingham, David Evans, Tal Malkin, and Dongyan Xu, editors, *Proceedings of the 2017 ACM SIGSAC Conference on Computer and Communications Security, CCS 2017, Dallas, TX, USA, October 30 - November 03, 2017*, pages 747–764. ACM, 2017.

[CTL97] Christian Collberg, Clark Thomborson, and Douglas Low. A taxonomy of obfuscating transformations. Technical report, Department of Computer Science, The University of Auckland, New Zealand, 1997.

[CV13] Ran Canetti and Vinod Vaikuntanathan. Obfuscating branching programs using black-box pseudo-free groups. Cryptology ePrint Archive, Report 2013/500, 2013. http://eprint.iacr.org/2013/500, Version: 20130815:072810.

[DDM16] Pratish Datta, Ratna Dutta, and Sourav Mukhopadhyay. Functional encryption for inner product with full function privacy. In Chen-Mou Cheng, Kai-Min Chung, Giuseppe Persiano, and Bo-Yin Yang, editors, *Public-Key Cryptography - PKC 2016 - 19th IACR International Conference on Practice and Theory in Public-Key Cryptography, Taipei, Taiwan, March 6-9, 2016, Proceedings, Part I*, volume 9614 of *Lecture Notes in Computer Science*, pages 164–195. Springer, 2016.

[Den02] Alexander W. Dent. Adapting the weaknesses of the random oracle model to the generic group model. In *Advances in Cryptology - ASIACRYPT 2002, 8th International Conference on the Theory and Application of Cryptology and Information Security, Queenstown, New Zealand, December 1-5, 2002, Proceedings*, pages 100–109, 2002.

[DGG+16] Nico Döttling, Sanjam Garg, Divya Gupta, Peihan Miao, and Pratyay Mukherjee. Obfuscation from low noise multilinear maps. Cryptology ePrint Archive, Report 2016/599, 2016. http://eprint.iacr.org/2016/599, Version: 20170619:052954.

[DH76] Whitfield Diffie and Martin E. Hellman. New directions in cryptography. *IEEE Trans. Information Theory*, 22(6):644–654, 1976.

[DLPR13] Cécile Delerablée, Tancrède Lepoint, Pascal Paillier, and Matthieu Rivain. White-box security notions for symmetric encryption schemes. In *Selected Areas in Cryptography - SAC 2013 - 20th International Conference, Burnaby, BC, Canada, August 14-16, 2013, Revised Selected Papers*, pages 247–264, 2013.

[DPM17]   Léo Ducas and Alice Pellet-Mary. On the statistical leak of the GGH13 multilinear map and some variants. Cryptology ePrint Archive, Report 2017/482, 2017. http://eprint.iacr.org/2017/482, Version: 20171106:092519.

[DSB17]   Denise Demirel, Lucas Schabhüser, and Johannes A. Buchmann. *Privately and Publicly Verifiable Computing Techniques - A Survey.* Springer Briefs in Computer Science. Springer, 2017.

[FHBNS16]   Marc Fischlin, Amir Herzberg, Hod Bin-Noon, and Haya Shulman. Obfuscation combiners. In *Advances in Cryptology - CRYPTO 2016 - 36th Annual International Cryptology Conference, Santa Barbara, CA, USA, August 14-18, 2016, Proceedings, Part II*, pages 521–550, 2016.

[FRS17]   Rex Fernando, Peter M. R. Rasmussen, and Amit Sahai. Preventing CLT attacks on obfuscation with linear overhead. In Tsuyoshi Takagi and Thomas Peyrin, editors, *Advances in Cryptology - ASIACRYPT 2017 - 23rd International Conference on the Theory and Applications of Cryptology and Information Security, Hong Kong, China, December 3-7, 2017, Proceedings, Part III*, volume 10626 of *Lecture Notes in Computer Science*, pages 242–271. Springer, 2017.

[FS90]   Uriel Feige and Adi Shamir. Witness indistinguishable and witness hiding protocols. In Harriet Ortiz, editor, *Proceedings of the 22nd Annual ACM Symposium on Theory of Computing, May 13-17, 1990, Baltimore, Maryland, USA*, pages 416–426. ACM, 1990.

[Gen09]   Craig Gentry. Fully homomorphic encryption using ideal lattices. In Michael Mitzenmacher, editor, *Proceedings of the 41st Annual ACM Symposium on Theory of Computing, STOC 2009, Bethesda, MD, USA, May 31 - June 2, 2009*, pages 169–178. ACM, 2009.

[Gen14]   Craig Gentry. Computing on the edge of chaos: Structure and randomness in encrypted computation. *Electronic Colloquium on Computational Complexity (ECCC)*, 21:106, 2014.

[GGG+14]   Shafi Goldwasser, S. Dov Gordon, Vipul Goyal, Abhishek Jain, Jonathan Katz, Feng-Hao Liu, Amit Sahai, Elaine Shi, and Hong-Sheng Zhou. Multi-input functional encryption. In Phong Q. Nguyen and Elisabeth Oswald, editors, *Advances in Cryptology - EURO-CRYPT 2014 - 33rd Annual International Conference on the Theory and Applications of Cryptographic Techniques, Copenhagen, Denmark, May 11-15, 2014. Proceedings*, volume 8441 of *Lecture Notes in Computer Science*, pages 578–602. Springer, 2014.

[GGH13a]   Sanjam Garg, Craig Gentry, and Shai Halevi. Candidate multilinear maps from ideal lattices. In Thomas Johansson and Phong Q. Nguyen, editors, *Advances in Cryptology - EUROCRYPT 2013, 32nd Annual International Conference on the Theory and Applications of Cryptographic Techniques, Athens, Greece, May 26-30, 2013. Proceedings*, volume 7881 of *Lecture Notes in Computer Science*, pages 1–17. Springer, 2013.

[GGH⁺13b] Sanjam Garg, Craig Gentry, Shai Halevi, Mariana Raykova, Amit Sahai, and Brent Waters. Candidate indistinguishability obfuscation and
functional encryption for all circuits. In *Foundations of Computer Science (FOCS), 2013 IEEE 54th Annual Symposium on*, pages 40–49.
IEEE, 2013.

[GGH15] Craig Gentry, Sergey Gorbunov, and Shai Halevi. Graph-induced multilinear maps from lattices. In *Theory of Cryptography - 12th Theory of
Cryptography Conference, TCC 2015, Warsaw, Poland, March 23-25,
2015, Proceedings, Part II*, pages 498–527, 2015.

[GGH⁺16] Sanjam Garg, Craig Gentry, Shai Halevi, Mariana Raykova, Amit Sahai, and Brent Waters. Hiding secrets in software: A cryptographic
approach to program obfuscation. *Commun. ACM*, 59(5):113–120,
April 2016.

[GGHW14] Sanjam Garg, Craig Gentry, Shai Halevi, and Daniel Wichs. On the
implausibility of differing-inputs obfuscation and extractable witness
encryption with auxiliary input. In *Advances in Cryptology - CRYPTO
2014 - 34th Annual Cryptology Conference, Santa Barbara, CA, USA,
August 17-21, 2014, Proceedings, Part I*, pages 518–535, 2014.

[GGHZ16] Sanjam Garg, Craig Gentry, Shai Halevi, and Mark Zhandry. Functional encryption without obfuscation. In Eyal Kushilevitz and Tal
Malkin, editors, *Theory of Cryptography - 13th International Conference, TCC 2016-A, Tel Aviv, Israel, January 10-13, 2016, Proceedings,
Part II*, volume 9563 of *Lecture Notes in Computer Science*, pages
480–511. Springer, 2016.

[GGJS13] Shafi Goldwasser, Vipul Goyal, Abhishek Jain, and Amit Sahai.
Multi-input functional encryption. Cryptology ePrint Archive, Report 2013/727, 2013. http://eprint.iacr.org/2013/727, Version: 20131113:052122.

[GGM86] Oded Goldreich, Shafi Goldwasser, and Silvio Micali. How to construct random functions. *J. ACM*, 33(4):792–807, 1986.

[GHRW14] Craig Gentry, Shai Halevi, Mariana Raykova, and Daniel Wichs. Out-
sourcing private RAM computation. In *55th IEEE Annual Symposium
on Foundations of Computer Science, FOCS 2014, Philadelphia, PA,
USA, October 18-21, 2014*, pages 404–413. IEEE Computer Society,
2014. Full version: http://eprint.iacr.org/2014/148.

[GIS⁺10] Vipul Goyal, Yuval Ishai, Amit Sahai, Ramarathnam Venkatesan, and
Akshay Wadia. Founding cryptography on tamper-proof hardware tokens. In *Theory of Cryptography, 7th Theory of Cryptography Conference, TCC 2010, Zurich, Switzerland, February 9-11, 2010. Proceedings*, pages 308–326, 2010.

[GK05] Shafi Goldwasser and Yael Tauman Kalai. On the impossibility of
obfuscation with auxiliary input. In *Foundations of Computer Science,
2005. FOCS 2005. 46th Annual IEEE Symposium on*, pages 553–562.
IEEE, 2005.

[GK16] Shafi Goldwasser and Yael Tauman Kalai. Cryptographic assumptions: A position paper. In *Theory of Cryptography - 13th International Conference, TCC 2016-A, Tel Aviv, Israel, January 10-13, 2016, Proceedings, Part I*, pages 505–522, 2016.

[GKP⁺13] Shafi Goldwasser, Yael Kalai, Raluca Ada Popa, Vinod Vaikuntanathan, and Nickolai Zeldovich. Reusable garbled circuits and succinct functional encryption. In *Proceedings of the Forty-fifth Annual ACM Symposium on Theory of Computing*, STOC '13, pages 555–564, New York, NY, USA, 2013. ACM.

[GLSW15] Craig Gentry, Allison Bishop Lewko, Amit Sahai, and Brent Waters. Indistinguishability obfuscation from the multilinear subgroup elimination assumption. In Venkatesan Guruswami, editor, *IEEE 56th Annual Symposium on Foundations of Computer Science, FOCS 2015, Berkeley, CA, USA, 17-20 October, 2015*, pages 151–170. IEEE Computer Society, 2015.

[GLW14] Craig Gentry, Allison B. Lewko, and Brent Waters. Witness encryption from instance independent assumptions. In *Advances in Cryptology - CRYPTO 2014 - 34th Annual Cryptology Conference, Santa Barbara, CA, USA, August 17-21, 2014, Proceedings, Part I*, pages 426–443, 2014.

[GM82] Shafi Goldwasser and Silvio Micali. Probabilistic encryption and how to play mental poker keeping secret all partial information. In *Proceedings of the 14th Annual ACM Symposium on Theory of Computing, May 5-7, 1982, San Francisco, California, USA*, pages 365–377, 1982.

[GMM⁺16] Sanjam Garg, Eric Miles, Pratyay Mukherjee, Amit Sahai, Akshayaram Srinivasan, and Mark Zhandry. Secure obfuscation in a weak multilinear map model. In Martin Hirt and Adam D. Smith, editors, *Theory of Cryptography - 14th International Conference, TCC 2016-B, Beijing, China, October 31 - November 3, 2016, Proceedings, Part II*, volume 9986 of *Lecture Notes in Computer Science*, pages 241–268, 2016.

[GMM17] Sanjam Garg, Mohammad Mahmoody, and Ameer Mohammed. When does functional encryption imply obfuscation? In Yael Kalai and Leonid Reyzin, editors, *Theory of Cryptography - 15th International Conference, TCC 2017, Baltimore, MD, USA, November 12-15, 2017, Proceedings, Part I*, volume 10677 of *Lecture Notes in Computer Science*, pages 82–115. Springer, 2017.

[GO96] Oded Goldreich and Rafail Ostrovsky. Software protection and simulation on oblivious rams. *J. ACM*, 43(3):431–473, 1996.

[Gol00] Oded Goldreich. Candidate one-way functions based on expander graphs. *Electronic Colloquium on Computational Complexity (ECCC)*, 7(90), 2000.

[Gol06] Oded Goldreich. *Foundations of Cryptography: Volume 1*. Cambridge University Press, New York, NY, USA, 2006.

[Gol08]   Oded Goldreich. *Computational Complexity: A Conceptual Perspective*. Cambridge University Press, New York, NY, USA, 1 edition, 2008.

[GR07]   Shafi Goldwasser and Guy N. Rothblum. On best-possible obfuscation. In *Theory of Cryptography, 4th Theory of Cryptography Conference, TCC 2007, Amsterdam, The Netherlands, February 21-24, 2007, Proceedings*, pages 194–213, 2007.

[GS14]   Divya Gupta and Amit Sahai. On constant-round concurrent zero-knowledge from a knowledge assumption. In *Progress in Cryptology - INDOCRYPT 2014 - 15th International Conference on Cryptology in India, New Delhi, India, December 14-17, 2014, Proceedings*, pages 71–88, 2014. Full version: http://eprint.iacr.org/2012/572.

[GS16]   Sanjam Garg and Akshayaram Srinivasan. Single-key to multi-key functional encryption with polynomial loss. In *Theory of Cryptography - 14th International Conference, TCC 2016-B, Beijing, China, October 31 - November 3, 2016, Proceedings, Part II*, pages 419–442, 2016.

[GSW13]   Craig Gentry, Amit Sahai, and Brent Waters. Homomorphic encryption from learning with errors: Conceptually-simpler, asymptotically-faster, attribute-based. In *Advances in Cryptology-CRYPTO 2013*, pages 75–92. Springer, 2013.

[GVW12]   Sergey Gorbunov, Vinod Vaikuntanathan, and Hoeteck Wee. Functional encryption with bounded collusions via multi-party computation. In *Advances in Cryptology - CRYPTO 2012 - 32nd Annual Cryptology Conference, Santa Barbara, CA, USA, August 19-23, 2012. Proceedings*, pages 162–179, 2012.

[GW11]   Craig Gentry and Daniel Wichs. Separating succinct non-interactive arguments from all falsifiable assumptions. In *Proceedings of the 43rd ACM Symposium on Theory of Computing, STOC 2011, San Jose, CA, USA, 6-8 June 2011*, pages 99–108, 2011.

[Had00]   Satoshi Hada. Zero-knowledge and code obfuscation. In *Advances in Cryptology-ASIACRYPT 2000*, pages 443–457. Springer, 2000.

[Hal15]   Shai Halevi. Graded encoding, variations on a scheme. Cryptology ePrint Archive, Report 2015/866, 2015. http://eprint.iacr.org/2015/866, Version: 20151030:192626.

[Her05]   Amir Herzberg. On tolerant cryptographic constructions. In Alfred Menezes, editor, *Topics in Cryptology - CT-RSA 2005, The Cryptographers' Track at the RSA Conference 2005, San Francisco, CA, USA, February 14-18, 2005, Proceedings*, volume 3376 of *Lecture Notes in Computer Science*, pages 172–190. Springer, 2005.

[HHSS17] Shai Halevi, Tzipora Halevi, Victor Shoup, and Noah Stephens-Davidowitz. Implementing BP-obfuscation using graph-induced encoding. In Bhavani M. Thuraisingham, David Evans, Tal Malkin, and Dongyan Xu, editors, *Proceedings of the 2017 ACM SIGSAC Conference on Computer and Communications Security, CCS 2017, Dallas,*

TX, USA, October 30 - November 03, 2017, pages 783–798. ACM, 2017.

[HJ16] Yupu Hu and Huiwen Jia. Cryptanalysis of GGH map. In Marc Fischlin and Jean-Sébastien Coron, editors, *Advances in Cryptology - EUROCRYPT 2016 - 35th Annual International Conference on the Theory and Applications of Cryptographic Techniques, Vienna, Austria, May 8-12, 2016, Proceedings, Part I*, volume 9665 of *Lecture Notes in Computer Science*, pages 537–565. Springer, 2016.

[HKN+05] Danny Harnik, Joe Kilian, Moni Naor, Omer Reingold, and Alon Rosen. On robust combiners for oblivious transfer and other primitives. In *Advances in Cryptology - EUROCRYPT 2005, 24th Annual International Conference on the Theory and Applications of Cryptographic Techniques, Aarhus, Denmark, May 22-26, 2005, Proceedings*, pages 96–113, 2005.

[HPS98] Jeffrey Hoffstein, Jill Pipher, and Joseph H. Silverman. NTRU: A ring-based public key cryptosystem. In Joe Buhler, editor, *Algorithmic Number Theory, Third International Symposium, ANTS-III, Portland, Oregon, USA, June 21-25, 1998, Proceedings*, volume 1423 of *Lecture Notes in Computer Science*, pages 267–288. Springer, 1998.

[HRSV11] Susan Hohenberger, Guy N. Rothblum, Abhi Shelat, and Vinod Vaikuntanathan. Securely obfuscating re-encryption. *J. Cryptology*, 24(4):694–719, 2011.

[HS10] Amir Herzberg and Haya Shulman. Robust combiners for software hardening. In *Trust and Trustworthy Computing, Third International Conference, TRUST 2010, Berlin, Germany, June 21-23, 2010. Proceedings*, pages 282–289, 2010.

[IK00] Yuval Ishai and Eyal Kushilevitz. Randomizing polynomials: A new representation with applications to round-efficient secure computation. In *41st Annual Symposium on Foundations of Computer Science, FOCS 2000, 12-14 November 2000, Redondo Beach, California, USA*, pages 294–304. IEEE Computer Society, 2000.

[Imp95] Russell Impagliazzo. A personal view of average-case complexity. In *Proceedings of the Tenth Annual Structure in Complexity Theory Conference, Minneapolis, Minnesota, USA, June 19-22, 1995*, pages 134–147. IEEE Computer Society, 1995.

[IP99] Russell Impagliazzo and Ramamohan Paturi. Complexity of k-SAT. In *Proceedings of the 14th Annual IEEE Conference on Computational Complexity, Atlanta, Georgia, USA, May 4-6, 1999*, pages 237–240. IEEE Computer Society, 1999.

[IPS15] Yuval Ishai, Omkant Pandey, and Amit Sahai. Public-coin differing-inputs obfuscation and its applications. In Yevgeniy Dodis and Jesper Buus Nielsen, editors, *Theory of Cryptography - 12th Theory of Cryptography Conference, TCC 2015, Warsaw, Poland, March 23-25, 2015, Proceedings, Part II*, volume 9015 of *Lecture Notes in Computer Science*, pages 668–697. Springer, 2015.

[JBF02] Matthias Jacob, Dan Boneh, and Edward W. Felten. Attacking an obfuscated cipher by injecting faults. In *Security and Privacy in Digital Rights Management, ACM CCS-9 Workshop, DRM 2002, Washington, DC, USA, November 18, 2002, Revised Papers*, pages 16–31, 2002.

[Jou00] Antoine Joux. A one round protocol for tripartite Diffie–Hellman. In Wieb Bosma, editor, *Algorithmic Number Theory, 4th International Symposium, ANTS-IV, Leiden, The Netherlands, July 2-7, 2000, Proceedings*, volume 1838 of *Lecture Notes in Computer Science*, pages 385–394. Springer, 2000.

[Jou02] Antoine Joux. The Weil and Tate pairings as building blocks for public key cryptosystems. In Claus Fieker and David R. Kohel, editors, *Algorithmic Number Theory, 5th International Symposium, ANTS-V, Sydney, Australia, July 7-12, 2002, Proceedings*, volume 2369 of *Lecture Notes in Computer Science*, pages 20–32. Springer, 2002.

[Kil88] Joe Kilian. Founding cryptography on oblivious transfer. In Janos Simon, editor, *Proceedings of the 20th Annual ACM Symposium on Theory of Computing, May 2-4, 1988, Chicago, Illinois, USA*, pages 20–31. ACM, 1988.

[KLW15] Venkata Koppula, Allison Bishop Lewko, and Brent Waters. Indistinguishability obfuscation for Turing machines with unbounded memory. In Rocco A. Servedio and Ronitt Rubinfeld, editors, *Proceedings of the Forty-Seventh Annual ACM Symposium on Theory of Computing, STOC 2015, Portland, OR, USA, June 14-17, 2015*, pages 419–428. ACM, 2015.

[KM07] Neal Koblitz and Alfred Menezes. Another look at generic groups. *Advances in Mathematics of Communications*, 1(1):13–28, 2007.

[KM15] Neal Koblitz and Alfred J. Menezes. The random oracle model: a twenty-year retrospective. *Des. Codes Cryptography*, 77(2-3):587–610, 2015.

[KNT17a] Fuyuki Kitagawa, Ryo Nishimaki, and Keisuke Tanaka. From single-key to collusion-resistant secret-key functional encryption by leveraging succinctness. Cryptology ePrint Archive, Report 2017/638, 2017. http://eprint.iacr.org/2017/638, Version: 20171012:050518.

[KNT17b] Fuyuki Kitagawa, Ryo Nishimaki, and Keisuke Tanaka. Indistinguishability obfuscation for all circuits from secret-key functional encryption. Cryptology ePrint Archive, Report 2017/361, 2017. http://eprint.iacr.org/2017/361, Version: 20171012:060224, To be published: IACR-EUROCRYPT-2018.

[KNT17c] Fuyuki Kitagawa, Ryo Nishimaki, and Keisuke Tanaka. Simple generic constructions of succinct functional encryption. Cryptology ePrint Archive, Report 2017/275, 2017. http://eprint.iacr.org/2017/275, Version: 20171012:052348.

[KNT18a] Fuyuki Kitagawa, Ryo Nishimaki, and Keisuke Tanaka. Obfustopia built on secret-key functional encryption. In Jesper Buus Nielsen and Vincent Rijmen, editors, *Advances in Cryptology - EUROCRYPT 2018*

- *37th Annual International Conference on the Theory and Applications of Cryptographic Techniques, Tel Aviv, Israel, April 29 - May 3, 2018 Proceedings, Part II*, volume 10821 of *Lecture Notes in Computer Science*, pages 603–648. Springer, 2018.

[KNT18b] Fuyuki Kitagawa, Ryo Nishimaki, and Keisuke Tanaka. Simple and generic constructions of succinct functional encryption. In Michel Abdalla and Ricardo Dahab, editors, *Public-Key Cryptography - PKC 2018 - 21st IACR International Conference on Practice and Theory of Public-Key Cryptography, Rio de Janeiro, Brazil, March 25-29, 2018, Proceedings, Part II*, volume 10770 of *Lecture Notes in Computer Science*, pages 187–217. Springer, 2018.

[KPTZ13] Aggelos Kiayias, Stavros Papadopoulos, Nikos Triandopoulos, and Thomas Zacharias. Delegatable pseudorandom functions and applications. In *2013 ACM SIGSAC Conference on Computer and Communications Security, CCS'13, Berlin, Germany, November 4-8, 2013*, pages 669–684, 2013.

[KS16] Ágnes Kiss and Thomas Schneider. Valiant's universal circuit is practical. In Marc Fischlin and Jean-Sébastien Coron, editors, *Advances in Cryptology - EUROCRYPT 2016 - 35th Annual International Conference on the Theory and Applications of Cryptographic Techniques, Vienna, Austria, May 8-12, 2016, Proceedings, Part I*, volume 9665 of *Lecture Notes in Computer Science*, pages 699–728. Springer, 2016.

[KSW13] Jonathan Katz, Amit Sahai, and Brent Waters. Predicate encryption supporting disjunctions, polynomial equations, and inner products. *J. Cryptology*, 26(2):191–224, 2013.

[Lev87] Leonid A. Levin. One way functions and pseudorandom generators. *Combinatorica*, 7(4):357–363, 1987.

[Lin16] Huijia Lin. Indistinguishability obfuscation from constant-degree graded encoding schemes. In Marc Fischlin and Jean-Sébastien Coron, editors, *Advances in Cryptology - EUROCRYPT 2016 - 35th Annual International Conference on the Theory and Applications of Cryptographic Techniques, Vienna, Austria, May 8-12, 2016, Proceedings, Part I*, volume 9665 of *Lecture Notes in Computer Science*, pages 28–57. Springer, 2016.

[Lin17] Huijia Lin. Indistinguishability obfuscation from SXDH on 5-linear maps and locality-5 PRGs. In Jonathan Katz and Hovav Shacham, editors, *Advances in Cryptology - CRYPTO 2017 - 37th Annual International Cryptology Conference, Santa Barbara, CA, USA, August 20-24, 2017, Proceedings, Part I*, volume 10401 of *Lecture Notes in Computer Science*, pages 599–629. Springer, 2017.

[LM16] Baiyu Li and Daniele Micciancio. Compactness vs collusion resistance in functional encryption. In *Theory of Cryptography - 14th International Conference, TCC 2016-B, Beijing, China, October 31 - November 3, 2016, Proceedings, Part II*, pages 443–468, 2016.

[LM18]   Huijia Lin and Christian Matt. Pseudo flawed-smudging generators
           and their application to indistinguishability obfuscation. Cryptology
           ePrint Archive, Report 2018/646, 2018. https://eprint.iacr.
           org/2018/646 Version:20180706:125509.

[LMA+16]   Kevin Lewi, Alex J. Malozemoff, Daniel Apon, Brent Carmer, Adam
           Foltzer, Daniel Wagner, David W. Archer, Dan Boneh, Jonathan Katz,
           and Mariana Raykova. 5Gen: A framework for prototyping appli-
           cations using multilinear maps and matrix branching programs. In
           Edgar R. Weippl, Stefan Katzenbeisser, Christopher Kruegel, An-
           drew C. Myers, and Shai Halevi, editors, *Proceedings of the 2016 ACM
           SIGSAC Conference on Computer and Communications Security, Vi-
           enna, Austria, October 24-28, 2016*, pages 981–992. ACM, 2016.

[LP09a]   Yehuda Lindell and Benny Pinkas. A proof of security of Yao's proto-
           col for two-party computation. *Journal of Cryptology*, 22(2):161–188,
           2009.

[LP09b]   Yehuda Lindell and Benny Pinkas. Secure multiparty computation for
           privacy-preserving data mining. *Journal of Privacy and Confidential-
           ity*, 1(1):5, 2009. Available at: http://repository.cmu.edu/jpc/
           vol1/iss1/5.

[LPS04]   Ben Lynn, Manoj Prabhakaran, and Amit Sahai. Positive results and
           techniques for obfuscation. In Christian Cachin and Jan Camenisch,
           editors, *Advances in Cryptology - EUROCRYPT 2004, International
           Conference on the Theory and Applications of Cryptographic Tech-
           niques, Interlaken, Switzerland, May 2-6, 2004, Proceedings*, volume
           3027 of *Lecture Notes in Computer Science*, pages 20–39. Springer,
           2004.

[LPST16a] Huijia Lin, Rafael Pass, Karn Seth, and Sidharth Telang. Indistin-
           guishability obfuscation with non-trivial efficiency. In Chen-Mou
           Cheng, Kai-Min Chung, Giuseppe Persiano, and Bo-Yin Yang, editors,
           *Public-Key Cryptography - PKC 2016 - 19th IACR International Con-
           ference on Practice and Theory in Public-Key Cryptography, Taipei,
           Taiwan, March 6-9, 2016, Proceedings, Part II*, volume 9615 of *Lec-
           ture Notes in Computer Science*, pages 447–462. Springer, 2016.

[LPST16b] Huijia Lin, Rafael Pass, Karn Seth, and Sidharth Telang. Output-
           compressing randomized encodings and applications. In Eyal Kushile-
           vitz and Tal Malkin, editors, *Theory of Cryptography - 13th Interna-
           tional Conference, TCC 2016-A, Tel Aviv, Israel, January 10-13, 2016,
           Proceedings, Part I*, volume 9562 of *Lecture Notes in Computer Sci-
           ence*, pages 96–124. Springer, 2016.

[LS14]   Hyung Tae Lee and Jae Hong Seo. Security analysis of multilinear
           maps over the integers. In Juan A. Garay and Rosario Gennaro, edi-
           tors, *Advances in Cryptology - CRYPTO 2014 - 34th Annual Cryptol-
           ogy Conference, Santa Barbara, CA, USA, August 17-21, 2014, Pro-
           ceedings, Part I*, volume 8616 of *Lecture Notes in Computer Science*,
           pages 224–240. Springer, 2014.

[LSS14] Adeline Langlois, Damien Stehlé, and Ron Steinfeld. GGHLite: More efficient multilinear maps from ideal lattices. In *Advances in Cryptology - EUROCRYPT 2014 - 33rd Annual International Conference on the Theory and Applications of Cryptographic Techniques, Copenhagen, Denmark, May 11-15, 2014. Proceedings*, pages 239–256, 2014.

[LT17] Huijia Lin and Stefano Tessaro. Indistinguishability obfuscation from trilinear maps and block-wise local PRGs. In Jonathan Katz and Hovav Shacham, editors, *Advances in Cryptology - CRYPTO 2017 - 37th Annual International Cryptology Conference, Santa Barbara, CA, USA, August 20-24, 2017, Proceedings, Part I*, volume 10401 of *Lecture Notes in Computer Science*, pages 630–660. Springer, 2017.

[LV16a] Huijia Lin and Vinod Vaikuntanathan. Indistinguishability obfuscation from DDH-like assumptions on constant-degree graded encodings. In *IEEE 57th Annual Symposium on Foundations of Computer Science, FOCS 2016, 9-11 October 2016, Hyatt Regency, New Brunswick, New Jersey, USA*, pages 11–20, 2016.

[LV16b] Huijia Lin and Vinod Vaikuntanathan. Indistinguishability obfuscation from DDH-like assumptions on constant-degree graded encodings. Cryptology ePrint Archive, Report 2016/795, 2016. http://eprint.iacr.org/2016/795, Version: 20170831:131738.

[LV17] Alex Lombardi and Vinod Vaikuntanathan. Minimizing the complexity of Goldreich's pseudorandom generator. Cryptology ePrint Archive, Report 2017/277, 2017. http://eprint.iacr.org/2017/277, Version: 20170327:014225.

[Mau05] Ueli M. Maurer. Abstract models of computation in cryptography. In *Cryptography and Coding, 10th IMA International Conference, Cirencester, UK, December 19-21, 2005, Proceedings*, pages 1–12, 2005.

[Mit15] Arno Andreas Mittelbach. *Random Oracles in the Standard Model.* PhD thesis, Technische Universität, Darmstadt, December 2015.

[MMN16] Mohammad Mahmoody, Ameer Mohammed, and Soheil Nematihaji. On the impossibility of virtual black-box obfuscation in idealized models. In Eyal Kushilevitz and Tal Malkin, editors, *Theory of Cryptography - 13th International Conference, TCC 2016-A, Tel Aviv, Israel, January 10-13, 2016, Proceedings, Part I*, volume 9562 of *Lecture Notes in Computer Science*, pages 18–48. Springer, 2016.

[MST06] Elchanan Mossel, Amir Shpilka, and Luca Trevisan. On epsilon-biased generators in NC^0. *Random Struct. Algorithms*, 29(1):56–81, 2006.

[MSW15] Eric Miles, Amit Sahai, and Mor Weiss. Protecting obfuscation against arithmetic attacks. Cryptology ePrint Archive, Report 2014/878, 2015. http://eprint.iacr.org/2014/878, Version: 20151201:190055.

[MSZ16] Eric Miles, Amit Sahai, and Mark Zhandry. Annihilation attacks for multilinear maps: Cryptanalysis of indistinguishability obfuscation over GGH13. In *Advances in Cryptology - CRYPTO 2016 - 36th Annual International Cryptology Conference, Santa Barbara, CA, USA, August 14-18, 2016, Proceedings, Part II*, pages 629–658, 2016.

[MW16] Pratyay Mukherjee and Daniel Wichs. Two round multiparty computation via multi-key FHE. In Marc Fischlin and Jean-Sébastien Coron, editors, *Advances in Cryptology - EUROCRYPT 2016 - 35th Annual International Conference on the Theory and Applications of Cryptographic Techniques, Vienna, Austria, May 8-12, 2016, Proceedings, Part II*, volume 9666 of *Lecture Notes in Computer Science*, pages 735–763. Springer, 2016.

[Nao03] Moni Naor. On cryptographic assumptions and challenges. In Dan Boneh, editor, *Advances in Cryptology - CRYPTO 2003, 23rd Annual International Cryptology Conference, Santa Barbara, California, USA, August 17-21, 2003, Proceedings*, volume 2729 of *Lecture Notes in Computer Science*, pages 96–109. Springer, 2003.

[Nec94] V. I. Nechaev. Complexity of a determinate algorithm for the discrete logarithm. *Mathematical Notes*, 55(2):165–172, Feb 1994.

[NY90] Moni Naor and Moti Yung. Public-key cryptosystems provably secure against chosen ciphertext attacks. In Harriet Ortiz, editor, *Proceedings of the 22nd Annual ACM Symposium on Theory of Computing, May 13-17, 1990, Baltimore, Maryland, USA*, pages 427–437. ACM, 1990.

[O'N10] Adam O'Neill. Definitional issues in functional encryption. Cryptology ePrint Archive, Report 2010/556, 2010. http://eprint.iacr.org/2010/556, Version: 20110319:050336.

[OT08] Tatsuaki Okamoto and Katsuyuki Takashima. Homomorphic encryption and signatures from vector decomposition. In *Pairing-Based Cryptography - Pairing 2008, Second International Conference, Egham, UK, September 1-3, 2008. Proceedings*, pages 57–74, 2008.

[OW14] Ryan O'Donnell and David Witmer. Goldreich's PRG: evidence for near-optimal polynomial stretch. In *IEEE 29th Conference on Computational Complexity, CCC 2014, Vancouver, BC, Canada, June 11-13, 2014*, pages 1–12, 2014.

[Pas13] Rafael Pass. Unprovable security of perfect NIZK and non-interactive non-malleable commitments. In *Theory of Cryptography - 10th Theory of Cryptography Conference, TCC 2013, Tokyo, Japan, March 3-6, 2013. Proceedings*, pages 334–354, 2013.

[Pei16] Chris Peikert. A decade of lattice cryptography. *Foundations and Trends in Theoretical Computer Science*, 10(4):283–424, 2016.

[PM76] Franco P. Preparata and David E. Muller. Efficient parallel evaluation of boolean expressions. *IEEE Transactions on Computers*, 25(5):548–549, 1976.

[PS15] Omer Paneth and Amit Sahai. On the equivalence of obfuscation and multilinear maps. Cryptology ePrint Archive, Report 2015/791, 2015. http://eprint.iacr.org/2015/791, Version: 20150813:170458.

[PS16] Rafael Pass and Abhi Shelat. Impossibility of VBB obfuscation with ideal constant-degree graded encodings. In *Theory of Cryptography - 13th International Conference, TCC 2016-A, Tel Aviv, Israel, January 10-13, 2016, Proceedings, Part I*, pages 3–17, 2016.

[PST14] Rafael Pass, Karn Seth, and Sidharth Telang. Indistinguishability obfuscation from semantically-secure multilinear encodings. In Juan A. Garay and Rosario Gennaro, editors, *Advances in Cryptology - CRYPTO 2014 - 34th Annual Cryptology Conference, Santa Barbara, CA, USA, August 17-21, 2014, Proceedings, Part I*, volume 8616 of *Lecture Notes in Computer Science*, pages 500–517. Springer, 2014.

[Rab79] M. O. Rabin. Digitalized signatures and public-key functions as intractable as factorization. Technical report, Cambridge, MA, USA, 1979.

[RAD78] Ronald L Rivest, Len Adleman, and Michael L Dertouzos. On data banks and privacy homomorphisms. *Foundations of secure computation*, 4(11):169–180, 1978.

[Reg05] Oded Regev. On lattices, learning with errors, random linear codes, and cryptography. In Harold N. Gabow and Ronald Fagin, editors, *Proceedings of the 37th Annual ACM Symposium on Theory of Computing, Baltimore, MD, USA, May 22-24, 2005*, pages 84–93. ACM, 2005.

[Ric53] H. G. Rice. Classes of recursively enumerable sets and their decision problems. *Transactions of the American Mathematical Society*, 74(2):358–366, 1953.

[Rot13] Ron Rothblum. On the circular security of bit-encryption. In *Theory of Cryptography - 10th Theory of Cryptography Conference, TCC 2013, Tokyo, Japan, March 3-6, 2013. Proceedings*, pages 579–598, 2013.

[RTV04] Omer Reingold, Luca Trevisan, and Salil P. Vadhan. Notions of reducibility between cryptographic primitives. In *Theory of Cryptography, First Theory of Cryptography Conference, TCC 2004, Cambridge, MA, USA, February 19-21, 2004, Proceedings*, pages 1–20, 2004.

[Sah14] Amit Sahai. How to encrypt a functionality (talk). Quantum Games and Protocols Workshop (Simons Institute, UC Berkeley), February 25. 2014. http://simons.berkeley.edu/talks/amit-sahai-2014-02-25, Accessed 20 Dec. 2017.

[Sha49] Claude E. Shannon. Communication theory of secrecy systems. *Bell System Technical Journal*, 28(4):656–715, 1949.

[Sho97] Victor Shoup. Lower bounds for discrete logarithms and related problems. In *Advances in Cryptology - EUROCRYPT '97, International Conference on the Theory and Application of Cryptographic Techniques, Konstanz, Germany, May 11-15, 1997, Proceeding*, pages 256–266, 1997.

[SKK+16] Sebastian Schrittwieser, Stefan Katzenbeisser, Johannes Kinder, Georg Merzdovnik, and Edgar R. Weippl. Protecting software through obfuscation: Can it keep pace with progress in code analysis? *ACM Comput. Surv.*, 49(1):4, 2016.

[SS10]   Amit Sahai and Hakan Seyalioglu. Worry-free encryption: functional encryption with public keys. In *Proceedings of the 17th ACM Conference on Computer and Communications Security, CCS 2010, Chicago, Illinois, USA, October 4-8, 2010*, pages 463–472, 2010.

[SS11]   Damien Stehlé and Ron Steinfeld. Making NTRU as secure as worst-case problems over ideal lattices. In Kenneth G. Paterson, editor, *Advances in Cryptology - EUROCRYPT 2011 - 30th Annual International Conference on the Theory and Applications of Cryptographic Techniques, Tallinn, Estonia, May 15-19, 2011. Proceedings*, volume 6632 of *Lecture Notes in Computer Science*, pages 27–47. Springer, 2011.

[SW14]   Amit Sahai and Brent Waters. How to use indistinguishability obfuscation: Deniable encryption, and more. In *Proceedings of the 46th Annual ACM Symposium on Theory of Computing*, STOC '14, pages 475–484, New York, NY, USA, 2014. ACM.

[SWP09] Amitabh Saxena, Brecht Wyseur, and Bart Preneel. Towards security notions for white-box cryptography. In Pierangela Samarati, Moti Yung, Fabio Martinelli, and Claudio Agostino Ardagna, editors, *Information Security, 12th International Conference, ISC 2009, Pisa, Italy, September 7-9, 2009. Proceedings*, volume 5735 of *Lecture Notes in Computer Science*, pages 49–58. Springer, 2009.

[Tur36]   Alan M. Turing. On computable numbers, with an application to the Entscheidungsproblem. *Proceedings of the London Mathematical Society*, 2(42):230–265, 1936.

[TZJ⁺16] Florian Tramèr, Fan Zhang, Ari Juels, Michael K. Reiter, and Thomas Ristenpart. Stealing machine learning models via prediction APIs. In *25th USENIX Security Symposium, USENIX Security 16, Austin, TX, USA, August 10-12, 2016*, pages 601–618, 2016.

[vDGHV10] Marten van Dijk, Craig Gentry, Shai Halevi, and Vinod Vaikuntanathan. Fully homomorphic encryption over the integers. In Henri Gilbert, editor, *Advances in Cryptology - EUROCRYPT 2010, 29th Annual International Conference on the Theory and Applications of Cryptographic Techniques, French Riviera, May 30 - June 3, 2010. Proceedings*, volume 6110 of *Lecture Notes in Computer Science*, pages 24–43. Springer, 2010.

[Wat09]   Brent Waters. Dual system encryption: Realizing fully secure IBE and HIBE under simple assumptions. In *Advances in Cryptology - CRYPTO 2009, 29th Annual International Cryptology Conference, Santa Barbara, CA, USA, August 16-20, 2009. Proceedings*, pages 619–636, 2009.

[Wat15]   Brent Waters. A punctured programming approach to adaptively secure functional encryption. In Rosario Gennaro and Matthew Robshaw, editors, *Advances in Cryptology - CRYPTO 2015 - 35th Annual Cryptology Conference, Santa Barbara, CA, USA, August 16-20,*

2015, Proceedings, Part II, volume 9216 of *Lecture Notes in Computer Science*, pages 678–697. Springer, 2015.

[Wee05] Hoeteck Wee. On obfuscating point functions. In *Proceedings of the thirty-seventh annual ACM symposium on Theory of computing*, pages 523–532. ACM, 2005.

[Weg87] Ingo Wegener. *The complexity of Boolean functions*. Wiley-Teubner, 1987.

[Weg00] Ingo Wegener. *Branching Programs and Binary Decision Diagrams*. Society for Industrial and Applied Mathematics, 2000.

[Wu15] David J. Wu. Fully homomorphic encryption: Cryptography's holy grail. *ACM Crossroads*, 21(3):24–29, 2015.

[Wys09] Brecht Wyseur. *White-Box Cryptography*. PhD thesis, Katholieke Universiteit Leuven, 2009.

[XZKL17] H. Xu, Y. Zhou, Y. Kang, and M. R. Lyu. On Secure and Usable Program Obfuscation: A Survey. *ArXiv e-prints*, October 2017. https://arxiv.org/abs/1710.01139.

[Yao82] Andrew C. Yao. Protocols for secure computations. In *Proceedings of the 23rd Annual Symposium on Foundations of Computer Science*, SFCS '82, pages 160–164, Washington, DC, USA, 1982. IEEE Computer Society.

[Yao86] Andrew C. Yao. How to generate and exchange secrets. In *Proceedings of the 27th Annual Symposium on Foundations of Computer Science*, SFCS '86, pages 162–167, Washington, DC, USA, 1986. IEEE Computer Society.

[Zim15] Joe Zimmerman. How to Obfuscate Programs Directly. In Elisabeth Oswald and Marc Fischlin, editors, *Advances in Cryptology - EUROCRYPT 2015*, volume 9057 of *Lecture Notes in Computer Science*, pages 439–467. Springer Berlin Heidelberg, 2015.

Printed in the United States
By Bookmasters